Rrashima Swaarup Verma is a senior corporate analyst with over twenty years of experience in the corporate world. She is currently senior director with a leading US-based business research and consulting organization.

Rrashima is also a best-selling author, columnist and poet as well as an award-winning speaker. She runs a very successful podcast on romance writing where she interviews authors, writers and poets. She has also participated in several leading literature festivals and moderated many prestigious panel discussions.

Over the years, Rrashima's writings on romance, humour, gender equality, social issues, relationships and parenting have been widely published in prominent national and international publications. She also won the Orange Flower Award, 2023, powered by Women's Web in the category of short fiction.

Rrashima loves travelling around the world and exploring different cultures. She is an ardent fitness enthusiast and also enjoys listening to Latin and jazz music. Rrashima lives with her family in Gurugram.

Praise for the Book

'As a paediatrician, I frequently see the struggles and triumphs that parents experience every day. This book is a comforting read that new mothers will find very relatable as they navigate the incredible and rewarding journey of motherhood.'

—**Dr Ajay Karkra**, associate director (paediatrics), Max Hospital, Gurugram

'Navigating the early phase of motherhood is a symphony of sacrifice and growth. Rrashima S. Verma masterfully encapsulates the essence of this transformative phase in this book. With eloquence and empathy, she unveils the intricate tapestry woven from the threads of sleep deprivation, the indispensable need for a robust support system and the delicate art of finding equilibrium amidst life's whirlwind.'

—**Dr Reena Sethi**,
international award-winning ophthalmologist,
co-founder, Arunodaya Deseret Eye Hospital,
honoured with the ISMICS Certificate of Appreciation,
as a Woman of Substance

'This is a witty and warm take on the precious yet difficult days of early motherhood. The advice and the insights are practical, but the real pleasure is in the personal anecdotes, which all new mothers (and even seasoned mothers) will relate to. Rrashima's writing is easy and breezy, which is possibly the most suitable for an already harried and overwhelmed new mum.'

—**Suparna Mitra**, CEO,
Watches and Wearables Division,
Titan Company Ltd

'Rrashima's eloquent writing masterfully captures the essence of parenting, from the chaos of diaper changes to the unexpected moments of joy and laughter. Her vivid storytelling and practical advice resonate deeply, reminding me of my wife's incredible resilience and boundless love as she steers our family with grace and a never-ending supply of caffeine. This book is a testament to the shared journey of parenting, offering laughter and wisdom while we navigate this beautifully chaotic adventure.'

—**Dennis George**, educationist,
navigator and leadership development mentor,
vice chairman, Shalom Group of Schools

Sleep, Support And Sanity

A Survivor's Guide to Early Motherhood

RRASHIMA SWAARUP VERMA

Om Books International

First published in 2024 by

Om Books International

Corporate & Editorial Office
A-12, Sector 64, Noida 201 301
Uttar Pradesh, India
Phone: +91 120 477 4100
Email: editorial@ombooks.com
Website: www.ombooksinternational.com

Sales Office
107, Ansari Road, Darya Ganj
New Delhi 110 002, India
Phone: +91 11 4000 9000
Email: sales@ombooks.com
Website: www.ombooks.com

ISBN: 978-93-5376-998-7

Printed in India

10 9 8 7 6 5 4 3 2 1

'My mother had a great deal of trouble with me, but I think she enjoyed it.'

—Mark Twain

Contents

And Just Like That, It All Began …

I once read somewhere, 'Mothers don't sleep. They just worry with their eyes closed.'

Let us start on this note.

The first thought I had when they held him up for me to see was pure pride. That this perfect, round, dimple-cheeked child was mine. That I had created him. Okay, there was no case of immaculate conception here but still … I was seeing him, my baby, for the very first time. I was insanely happy. And he was beautiful. Oh yes, he was! Believe me, I am not saying this simply because I am his mother. I know, I know. All mothers look at their children through rose-tinted glasses, but he *really* was a beautiful baby—clear sharp features, upturned nose, the cutest little hands and feet. It might be worth mentioning here that my bestie later confessed to me that it was when she saw my baby for the first time that she decided to have one too. My delivery date and her conception date are the same. What a coincidence!

My grandfather on seeing my baby for the first time said, 'He has beautiful lips. He will be kissed by many women.' My gorgeous baby, a ladies' man! Well, I was not complaining.

I have to confess. I was anything but maternal in my previous avatar; in fact, I was 'extremely child-unfriendly'. I dreaded seeing children in restaurants, movie theatres, on flights, just about anywhere in public. There was a time when I firmly believed that children were to be seen and not heard and had no qualms about saying it too. I distinctly remember this one time when I was having dinner with my husband, Puneet, in an elegant Japanese restaurant and this child was loitering around near us. I tried glaring at him, tried catching his mother's eye, even commented loudly, 'how some people think it is okay to unleash their children on poor unsuspecting strangers'. All in vain though. But it was when the kid came right up to me and stuck his dirty little finger into the kappa ebisen basket (that is a Japanese prawn cracker by the way), that I completely lost it.

'Shoo!' I waved a hand at him, as though trying to swat an annoying fly. '*Shoo*!'

There was pin-drop silence in the restaurant. Even Puneet looked embarrassed. The child's mother, furious, asked, 'How *dare* you "shoo" him like that! He's not an insect. Have you never seen a child before?'

'Why the *hell* did you bring a child to a fine-dining Japanese restaurant?' I retorted irately. You see, the mothers and the non-mothers are two warring sides. And it was my duty to stick up for my side.

'It's not like he's crazy about sushi, is he? Little spoilt brat! Ruined my dinner!'

You get the picture, right? Now please don't ask me when I decided to switch over to the other side because I don't really remember. I suppose I must have had some sort of a 'maternal instinct' hidden deep within me which I *clearly* was not really aware of because when I saw my baby for the first time I experienced my very first brush with euphoria. I simply could not stop staring at Eshan's small chest rising and falling rhythmically, his eyes tightly shut, his dimpled hands curled up into tiny fists by his ears. I have heard that those first moments are supposed to be magical and blissful. Like something you have never experienced. That first time when your eyes meet, that first touch. It is oddly…familiar. As though, you have always known each other. There is also a strangeness to that first moment, as though suddenly you are in a world of your own where no one other than your baby exists. Enjoy those first moments to their fullest, be as starry-eyed as you want, stare at your little bundle of joy for as long as you wish to, sigh as many times as you feel like and smile that beatific, blissful smile that only a new mum can. Trust me, no one is going to judge you. You are a brand new mum after all …

Now to the brass tacks. When the initial feeling of bliss wears off (oh yes it does), the first thing you feel is total and complete exhaustion. I mean, think of what your body has been through to pop that little living, breathing, crying, kicking being into the world. Add to that nine months without caffeine plus a couple of sleepless nights and boy! *Does the euphoria wear off*! And how! For all the expectant mothers out there, please do not paint *any* rosy picture in your minds. Don't think that your babies will be these perfect little creatures who will cry on schedule, eat on schedule, poop on schedule. That they will be generous with their smiles and sleep through the night. Reality though is a far cry. And for God's sake, do not decide *not* to listen to other people's experiences. It is naive to think: *I don't know what other babies do. My baby would never do that.*

Yeah right! You wish.

The thing is that most newborns do not sleep well initially and most new parents do not really know what to do about it. It is not that we do not try; in fact, new parents try everything. *Everything.* We take the mittens off, we put the mittens on. We take the blanket off, we put the blanket on. We switch the A/C off, we switch the A/C on. On-off, on-off. Off-on, off-on. Seriously, who came up with that term '*sleep like a baby*'? It did not make sense, certainly not to my husband and me while we literally *begged* our newborn to calm down. And just as you would expect, the more we begged, the more he howled. The more he howled, the more we begged. And round and round we went. So much so that by the time the early morning light was filtering in through the thin cotton drapes at the window and the sun was opening up like a flower on the horizon on that first morning, Puneet and I were literally ready to kill each other. It is amazing how we never realize the importance of a good night's sleep until we have to go without it. Well-meaning friends and relatives had mentioned that it made sense to adapt my schedule with the baby's but frankly, after that first night, I had doubts whether anything would work. Yes, admittedly I was elated, uncertain and terrified all at once that first morning. If ever I had experienced a myriad concoction of different emotions, *that* was the moment. Phew!

What is worse than a night without sleep? A night without sleep followed by a morning of fresh-faced, bright-eyed relatives and friends *pouring* in to meet the newborn. Now you may love your near and dear ones to the moon and back and while it is wonderful to have everyone suddenly fussing over you, you really cannot help but wonder why they chose that *exact* moment to drop in when your apple of the eye was kind enough to have finally dozed off. Then there are those who insist on taking dozens of selfics with the new mum and baby. No matter if the new mum looks like she has never combed her hair or taken a shower in her life! But then, little does she know that combing hair and showering have become luxuries now. Thankfully, my parents and best friend, Simone, were the first ones to arrive that first morning. They tiptoed into the room, complete with a change of clothes and a huge flask of my favourite iced black coffee, which I almost snatched out of my bestie's hand. I am a coffee addict but had not allowed myself so much as a sip throughout my pregnancy.

'Thanks for this!'

I shot a grateful smile at Simone who had turned her attention to my baby and was making all kinds of cooing sounds to him.

'It wasn't easy mind you,' she said then, rolling her eyes. 'They're crazy in this hospital. No flowers, no balloons, no outside food! I managed to sneak it in somehow. But then, don't I always?'

She looked at me smugly.

'Hello, long-lost friend,' I muttered to the flask as I took my very first sip in nine months. Sighing contentedly, I leaned back on the pillows.

'Enjoy it while you can.' Simone smirked. 'There's a whole bunch of relatives about to storm into this room in minutes! I saw them all in the parking lot. In-laws, *maasi*, *bua*, *chacha*, *chachi* ...'

I looked at her in horror. I know we Indians are adept at handling a train of relatives at the most inopportune of times but my hair was a bird's nest perched on top of my head *and* I was having my very first coffee in nine months! I deserved some peace and quiet, right? As though on cue, my little one suddenly started bawling. Mothers and babies certainly do have a connection. We can *feel* each other's distress. Or maybe he too just wanted to comb his hair. Come to think of it, he had quite a lot of that for a newborn.

'Is *everyone* coming?' I asked weakly.

'Don't worry.'

My dad was quick to assure me.

'I've got the sanitizer ready.'

He produced a gigantic bottle from the bag he was holding and I sighed in relief. Sanitizers are life savers the moment you have a baby. In the days to come, I would realize that I might step out of the house without my lipstick or sunglasses but never without my bottle of sanitizer.

'And we've clearly told everyone that they can't stay more than ten minutes.' My mum patted my hand. 'You and the baby need rest.'

Thank God for mums! Honestly, if there is ever a time in a woman's life when she realizes the true worth of her mother, it is when she becomes a mother herself. More on that later.

'So, do you want to change the baby's clothes before the family arrives?' asked Mum.

She smiled at me and started pulling out a pile of gorgeous baby clothes out of the bag she was carrying. There were rompers and bodysuits in all colours of the rainbow, little caps, booties, leggings, mittens. I looked at the clothes in delight, suddenly remembering the many memorable Sunday afternoons my husband and I had spent in the peaceful aisles of maternity stores, shopping for our baby together. Afterwards, we would sit in a cafe, surrounded with colourful bags, sipping iced tea or strawberry smoothies and talking animatedly about all the things we could not wait to do with the baby. Even as the memory came rushing back to me, Puneet and I exchanged a smile. It seemed like he had the exact same thought.

'Jesus! Did you buy up the mall or something?' Simone's voice broke the reverie. She was staring at the growing pile of clothes in astonishment.

'Wait until you become a mum.'

I gave her a superior look and picked up a soft, downy, cornflower-blue babygro. Holding it against my cheek, I stroked the garment lovingly.

'Okay guys!' Puneet suddenly stood up, trying to stifle a huge yawn. 'Now that everyone's coming, I think I'll pop over to the house,' he said. 'And check my emails in case there's something urgent.'

Yeah right! All he really wanted to do was snuggle into bed, take a nice, long nap and forget that he had just become a father. Men! Aargh! But I smiled and waved him out of the room because quite frankly, one sleep-deprived, weary person was better than two.

So anyway, our first day with Eshan was fraught with activity and emotion. Exciting, exhausting and revelatory all at once. In a nutshell, the first day was bedlam. Don't get me wrong. There was utter joy every time I looked at my wee one, but hesitation and uncertainty about everything I was doing and bafflement at the sheer number of people who were suddenly around me. Honestly, they were *literally, constantly,* pouring into the 8 ft by 12 ft hospital room in droves—nurses, doctors, relatives, friends, colleagues, prospective nannies.

As for me, I was desperate to sleep and rest, but amazingly active and alert at the same time, and crazily possessive about my bundle of joy. Now when was the last time I cared this deeply about anyone? *Never*. I winced every time anyone picked my baby up, cringed when the baby nurse did something as simple as change his diaper and shuddered with relief when she finally put him back in the cot.

I will never forget that moment when the doctor came in to examine my baby for the first time after the birth and declared him perfectly healthy. It was such a tremendous relief! Like most parents, we conducted our own detailed examinations later, and marvelled at every tiny feature, peered at every little wrinkle and spot, and basically drove everyone else crazy. After all, I was a new mother. It was my job to strong-arm people into seeing how amazing my baby was. But then, the madness had only just begun …

'There is only one pretty child in the world, and every mother has it.'—Chinese proverb

1

Sleep, Support And Sanity

The Magic Words ...

'The quickest way for a parent to get a child's attention is to sit down and look comfortable.'

—Lane Olinghouse

What is the best way to test a perfectly rational, normal and pleasant woman's endurance? Make her go without sleep for a couple of nights and then expect her to hold a nine-pounder in her arms and sing nursery rhymes. You will see her being reduced to an incomprehensible, incoherent mess within a matter of minutes. It is common knowledge that the battle to get enough sleep is the bane of every new mum's life. Multiple feedings, diaper changes and trying, futilely mind you, to calm a screaming baby at 3 a.m.

is enough to turn any woman into someone she herself does not want to know. Did you know that studies have shown that sleeping less than five hours a night results in alertness equivalent to that of a legally drunk driver? Now that we have established the seriousness of this situation, bear with me.

'Sleep when the *baby sleeps.*'

We have all heard this 'pearl of wisdom' at some point, haven't we? Okay then, first the good news. With careful observation, analysis and coordination, quite a lot of this can be achieved. Because every baby does indeed have a schedule and adapting yours to your baby's will give you a lot of extra time to do the things you want to. For instance, you might have once been the first one to hit your neighbourhood gym every morning but if your baby sleeps at 3 a.m. every night, you may want to start considering an evening workout instead. You could tell yourself that muscle function peaks after sunset as do strength and performance. Be flexible and make those adjustments to your schedule and sleep cycle if you have to. It is all totally worth it. In a nutshell, just um … keep an open mind.

Naturally, it is not always as easy as it sounds. *Why*? Well, firstly, a baby's sleep cycle is not always 100 per cent predictable. Then again, not everyone can fall asleep on a dime. In fact, quite often the reverse is true. And finally, wonderful though this advice might be, it does kind of assume that new parents have *absolutely no other responsibilities* besides caring for their newborn. You might have an older child for example. How are you supposed to sleep when your older one is waiting to be taken to tae kwon do class? Or you might be at work for Christ's sake! You cannot say, client presentation be damned, this is my nap time! I do not think any boss would understand, however compassionate they might be.

Moving on, we were in the hospital for three nights. I concede that there are advantages of staying longer in the hospital as a baby nurse comes when you call and meals are served in bed. I also have friends who have even stayed longer than necessary simply because they are too terrified at the thought of managing their newborns without an army of professional help.

I, on the other hand, have never really had a thing for hospitals and by the end of the third day, Puneet and I were desperate to go home. I suppose the fact that our baby did not sleep at all during that time (or at least that is what it felt like to us since I am pretty sure he must have sneaked in what he needed while we were busy entertaining the throngs of relatives and friends) might have had something to do with our desperation to go home. As illogical as it feels now, at that time we were convinced that our baby would sleep better at home. I even remember telling Puneet (and quite emphatically so) that it had something to do with the hospital crib and that as soon as we would get home and I would lay him into the soft, white cradle with inbuilt moonlight and Beethoven music that I had bought for him, he would fall asleep instantly. I know! I know! A new mum will tell herself anything, but I did not know that then.

And so, we checked ourselves out of the hospital room on the fourth day and drove home with our baby and our brand new status of 'new parents' clearly displayed in the proud, wide smiles that we wore on our faces. Isn't there something absolutely lovely about entering your home with your baby for the very first time? The house was filled with flowers that our friends and family had sent over, the walls were festooned with red and blue balloons and there was a huge cake waiting on a silver stand. As we walked through the main door and into the nursery we had so lovingly readied for Eshan, I stroked his soft, downy head and inhaled his sweet, baby scent. His tiny fingers closed upon mine and I brought my lips close to his ear and gently whispered, 'Welcome home.'

Understandably, once the initial excitement of being back home had worn off a little, I realized that it was not all peaches and cream. To start with, the hospital nanny was no longer a bell away and Eshan did not sleep through the night in spite of the maestro's music. As for me, despite a crash course at the hospital by the baby nurse, I simply could not remember a damn thing about caring for a newborn. So, I looked at Mum for support, and she informed me in a shaky tone, 'I have completely forgotten everything about newborns!'

Can you imagine? How could *she*?

Okay, okay things *had* changed drastically in the world of newborns over the years, but *still*.

'Ma, you must remember *something*! Like, how to swaddle a baby for instance. Or mix a feed correctly. Or even how to change a diaper!'

'They didn't have diapers back then.'

Mum replied with a deadpan expression on her face.

Jesus! How did they even manage to survive without diapers?

'Okay, did you guys get any sleep at all?'

This was fast becoming the first question my husband and I were asked each morning.

'Actually, it was not such a bad night. We got a full hour.'

Puneet would reply, smile at me sardonically and then proceed to pour us both humungous mugs of coffee. Despite my own exhaustion, I could not help feeling sorry for him because I was still on maternity leave, but he had to go to work and then *pretend* to work. I would have actually told him to leave the nightly routine to me since I could still catch a nap during the day but he was insistent about doing his bit.

In hindsight, I have to say that despite the erratic sleep cycle, there was something special, almost enchanting about those sleepless nights. Whispering to each other like children in the dark as though we were sharing a secret, taking turns at holding our baby, singing 'Edelweiss' to him rather tunelessly (at least I tried; Puneet clearly preferred the music system).

'Well, at any rate I can drink coffee again,' I would shrug and gratefully accept the mug of black coffee from Puneet. 'Thank God for small mercies.'

Coming back to Mum …

She smiled at me kindly and replied, 'Oh, he'll start sleeping through the night eventually …'

Eventually? *Eventually*! What did 'eventually' even mean?

'You mean, *eventually,* I won't be watching crappy television at 3 a.m.! That *eventually,* I'll be able to go to bed at a normal time like everyone else and lie horizontal for eight straight hours. That's certainly good to know.'

Sleep is for the weak, the strong change diapers at 3 a.m.

I smiled wryly at my mum.

'Let him sleep with me twice a week.'

Hallelujah! I almost wept in relief. I loved Mum, of course, but at that moment I felt like throwing rose petals on the floor wherever she walks.

Eventually, plans were made to go out to dinner, watch a movie *and* finish a bottle of wine, all in the same evening. As expected, they were quickly discarded because we never could keep ourselves awake long enough. In fact, it would not be an exaggeration to say that I found myself falling asleep *anytime*, *anywhere,* during those first few weeks. In the beginning I thought it was kind of funny but I soon realized that it was a common problem when I read about a new mum who actually fell asleep while the dentist was drilling inside her mouth! Then there was this particularly exhausted father who was so sleep-deprived that he put the pacifier into his wife's mouth instead of the baby's. And she was so sleep-deprived herself, poor woman, that *she actually took it*, no questions asked. It is no wonder then that new parents are the easiest to spot anywhere? What are the dead giveaways, you may ask?

The bloodshot eyes and dazed expressions. *What else*?

Does this mean that new mums should just give up on getting a good night's sleep every once in a while? Not at all. We have to keep trying and hoping, and hoping and trying. Oh, did you know that babies sleep better with a bit of white noise in the background? Yup, all that tiptoeing around like ninjas that we new parents resort to *and* make others resort to is really unnecessary and quite the reverse of what we should be doing. So what is this white noise? It is basically consistent sounds coming out evenly across all hearable frequencies.

Too technical? Okay, to put it simply, it is just sounds that are generated naturally in an environment. Like a running tap or the whirring of the vacuum cleaner or even the sound of rain. White noise apparently soothes babies and helps them sleep and these days you can even get a white noise machine and place it in your baby's room to help him doze off. This certainly sounds more promising than Beethoven's music!

Okay, so what happens when nothing works? Well, one can always get professional help. No, I am not talking about a shrink (though that is not entirely ruled out for new parents trying to preserve their sanity). Right now, I am talking about the paediatric sleep consultants. Yes, yes, since angels could not be on earth we have such people in the world. I did not know until I became a mum. They are basically well, just what the name suggests. They are experts at sleep training and at counselling new parents on how to get through the newborn days as alert and refreshed as possible. They focus on things like a relaxing routine before bedtime, creating a peaceful sleep environment, co-sleeping (this will save a lot of night time trips to the nursery), accepting help when it is offered, infant sleep training, guiding you to take a power nap when you can and not ignoring signs of serious sleep debt. Basically, all *very* doable things. Try them all out and see what works. As long as you get some of that magic S-word, it is worth it.

Now that professional help is sorted, let us talk a little about the other kind of help. You know, the kind that comes from a spouse, mums and dads, friends and family. Needless to say, the people who will come to your rescue during those first few months are the ones you will remember with unconditional gratitude for the rest of your lives. Even that particularly belligerent sister-in-law whom you could not stand before. You might see yourself thawing towards her because she helped you out during this extremely needy phase of your life. So what if she was behind that awful misunderstanding between you and your husband, that had you frantically hunting for divorce lawyers on Google the next day! Even if she comes over to babysit your child twice a week, you could wash your hair and catch a nap and that is all that matters!

These were the people who bailed you out when you were so beside yourself with sheer exhaustion that you could not even remember your own name! They were the ones who helped you preserve your sanity when you were ready to tear every strand of your hair out! They say it takes a village to raise a child, but modern systems of living have changed all that. With family very often living on the other side of the country or even the world, indifferent neighbours, friends who would love to help but do not have the time and experience to do it and efficient, honest nannies increasingly becoming as rare as four-leafed clovers, it is not a surprise that many mums suffer from fatigue, stress, depression and loneliness. There are, however, some basic things that new mums can do to make the journey easier. These are not professional guidelines, just easy, honest, simple tips from one mum to another.

Enlist your partner's help

He is your significant other. If he is not going to help out, who will? And frankly, not only does it give the new mum a respite, the dad gets to bond with his baby too. A study revealed that a father's involvement during the first few weeks after delivery, can help strengthen family bonding for years after. If that is not reason enough, what is? All you need to do is to manage your schedules a bit better than before to ensure that the baby care coordinates with your spouse's work commitments *and* you are able to use the help whenever possible. Puneet for instance, was able to tweak his schedule and get home a little earlier in the evenings. That allowed him to catch a nap and then do the night feeds while I got some rest. I would in turn, wake up early and handle the morning so that he could sleep in before heading to work.

Join a mummy support group

During this life-changing phase of your life, it is extremely important to know that you are not alone in the journey. Parks, activity groups and play areas are great places to meet other mums who are in similar stages of life. You can share notes and ideas, suggest solutions and give each other the emotional support that only others in the same situation can. Obviously, a structured support group is a great idea but even a simple heart-to-heart talk with another mum can help. Sometimes you do not even have to do anything, just being there for each other is enough.

I simply must share this one particular incident with you. There was this time when I was completely, utterly sleep-deprived. I did not get a decent night's sleep in a week. Hence, I was constantly irritable, cranky and snappy. One evening, I went to the playground with my son and there she was. Another mum who had fifty shades of dark circles under her eyes. She was a complete stranger but honestly, at that time, we were like kindred spirits. Just looking at her weary face and sluggish eyes and listening to her talk about how her son had kept her awake the previous night, made me feel like I was not the only one. It gave me the comfort that I needed. 'You can say it to me. I'm a mother too.' Just hearing that can soothe you like nothing else can.

Delegate, delegate; outsource, outsource

There is no perfectly synchronized support system out there, but there are plenty of things which can be delegated or outsourced to make our lives easier. For instance, even if you enjoy cooking dinner daily, would it not be better to get someone to do the cooking and use that time to spend with your baby or wash your hair instead? Another thing that can be a new mummy's best friend during this time-deficient phase of her life, is online shopping. It is the ultimate answer, at least for things that do not require too much physical examination right from groceries to gadgets. Is there any point packing a diaper bag and strapping a wailing baby into a car seat just to get some toilet paper?

Seize every opportunity to do a little something for yourself

Being a new mum can be overwhelming. So much so, that you can easily forget that you exist too, so you will need to keep reminding yourself of that. Take care of your own needs. Make some time for yourself even if it is just 15 minutes. Get out of the house when you can. Get a babysitter (could be your mum or friend) for a couple of hours, make the most of that time. Do not use that time to do the laundry or cook a meal. Laundry can wait. Meals can be ordered in. Give yourself the much needed *me* time. Grab a coffee with a friend, make an appointment at the salon, hit the gym, get some retail therapy (definitely cheaper than seeing a shrink) or just take a nap. A happy, relaxed mother will raise a happy, relaxed child.

Try not to feel guilty about everything

Yes, we are mums now, yes we are responsible for the well-being of a tiny, crying, kicking but incredibly adorable bundle of joy but believe it or not, even mums do not have to jump up every time their babies bat an eyelid. The truth is that, along with you, your baby benefits from some downtime too. Very often a baby does not even want any attention, he is perfectly happy on his own, staring at the ceiling. So, do not overstress. It is perfectly all right to let a few things slide every once in a while. You have got a lovely baby, you cannot also have a spotless house and an impeccable garden all the time. Difficult though it is, try not to pressurise yourself about maintaining a perfect house, managing your work and meeting your child's every need, every moment of every day. It is perplexing how perfectly reasonable, relaxed women turn into these frenzied, overdriven perfectionists as soon as they become mums. It is almost as though they are constantly testing and challenging themselves to see how much more they can fit into an already frenetic life.

Is this a race or a competition on who breastfeeds the longest or who knows more nursery rhymes or even who manages to get home in time to take her baby to the park every single evening? No, right? This is about enjoying your baby, managing to shower every day and holding on to your sanity …

2

When? What? Why? Where? How?

My All-time Favourite Questions!

'There is no way to be a perfect mother, and a million ways to be a good one.'

— Jill Churchill

'Sometimes I feel like I'm murmuring a volley of questions in my sleep,' remarked my friend. 'My mum calls me a walking, talking questionnaire. But I guess that's to be expected. I'm a new mother…'

Now this particular friend and I had a rather interesting start to our friendship. We met for the very first time in the most unforgettable of places—the delivery room. Our children are exactly an hour apart. Not surprisingly, we developed an instant bond. How could we not? We were going through similar experiences for the first time. And one thing that both of us definitely had in common was a questionnaire that was as never-ending, perplexing and varied as anything could be.

We officially entered a fascinating new world full of shifting, conflicting emotions and remarkable, spellbinding experiences. It felt like we enrolled into a crash course in learning how to handle ... well, pretty much everything that we were clueless about. They say, one learns best through one's experiences and one of the best examples of that is new motherhood. However, that does not stop us from asking everyone who cares to listen a plethora of questions and seeking a multitude of reassuring answers. I would rather be silly than sorry. Yes, we ask a trillion questions, many of them irrelevant. Yes, we seek clarifications and assurances and reassurances almost all the time but what the hell! We are new mothers! The first few months of life are crucial to the baby's safety and health, so we must not let hesitation or embarrassment get in the way. Since babies do not come with a manual, even the thought of being completely responsible for this precious, tiny bundle can be overwhelmingly frightening. We want to know what is normal, what is safe and what is not. Let me clarify, that does not mean that we welcome unsolicited advice *all the time* because we don't. Just because we asked for a couple of easy-to-blend fruit recipes does not mean that we want to hear a half-hour lecture about how everything we are doing is wrong! C'mon, new motherhood is a baffling time! Being a mum is the one job that demands everything you have got and that is as arduous as it is soul-satisfying. So, it is natural to want to talk to people who have more experience and can offer practical advice to make things as easy as possible. The key word here is trust. It is best for a new mother to seek advice from people she trusts because that is the advice she will instinctively follow through.

'When do babies start sleeping through the night?'

This was my undisputed 'No. 1' question throughout the first year for obvious reasons. Then, of course, there are the other common ones that most new mothers ask.

'Do I really have to breastfeed for a full year?'

'Is it bad to wake a sleeping baby?'

'Can I drink wine while breastfeeding?'

'Is swaddling necessary?'

'How long does teething pain last?'

'How long will he wear diapers?'

'Why does her nose get blocked at night?'

'Does she have colic?'

The why's, when's, what's, how's become a part of daily conversation as we tentatively navigate our ways through unfamiliar paths, trying to get answers to those deep, confounding mysteries, all the time petrified of making a mistake. It might be worth mentioning here that several of these questions may even be those that we constantly ask *ourselves*, secret conversations that we have in our minds in those moments of utter despair. You know, like those 3 a.m. conversations except that these occur *all the time*.

The thing to remember is that questions, doubts, clarifications, uncertainties, fears and reassurance are all a part of this journey, which I must add is a very rewarding learning experience. A journey which very often even goes on to become a sort of role reversal when *we* become the veterans, generously doling out advice to brand-new, anxious, sleep-deprived mums. The person asking the question and the one answering can change, but the questions don't. The questions, an integral part of the experience of new parenthood, stay, passed on from one to the other, almost like a legacy. So how can we make this soul-searching, answer-seeking journey a little easier, a little less confounding for ourselves?

Find or form a parent support group

There is really nothing like talking to others in a similar situation. As they say, we are all in the same boat. Yes, sometimes the others are as baffled, as anxious, as sceptical or simply just as clueless as we are, but just sharing, talking, discussing with someone who empathizes, understands, basically *gets it*, can give the answers. And, since each person's experience is unique, a new mum can get a preview of all the variables she can expect rather than a more general point of view. The good news is that support groups are very common these days. They could be informal ones where a group of neighbourhood mums meet thrice a week to chat about minor issues like burping, swaddling and teething, or a slightly more structured one where you talk about sleeping patterns and exchange recipes on how to disguise broccoli so that your child will eat it, or even the most organized ones where you go all the way and discuss serious issues like post-partum depression (PPD) and the like. As long as the support group is there, go right ahead and join. And if you cannot find one that is suitable, form your own.

Talk to your paediatrician

It is amazing how many of our questions can be answered without too much hullabaloo if we are simply lucky enough to have a knowledgeable and understanding paediatrician. There is very little a new parent can't ask the paediatrician. Speaking for myself, I cannot even begin to count the number of times that talking to my child's paediatrician has helped me get answers. To give him credit, he has always been extremely accommodating. I recall one particularly funny incident. Eshan was a couple of weeks old, and a thought came to me sometime in the wee hours of the morning. After what seemed like an excruciatingly long wait, I called his doctor as soon as the clock struck nine.

'He cries a lot, but not a single tear comes out. When I cry, it seems as though someone has turned on a tap. We have the same genes, Doctor. Why doesn't he cry proper tears? Is he just pretending to cry or something?'

The doctor was as patient as ever. 'First of all, tears have nothing to do with genes,' he said in a matter-of-fact tone. I am sure trying hard to conceal his amusement. 'A newborn's tear ducts take several weeks to develop. Nothing to worry about, Rrashima. It's all good.'

With a huge sigh of relief, I thanked the doctor and went back to my work.

If you read back to some of the commonest questions asked by new parents, you will see that most of them can be easily answered by your child's paediatrician. Perhaps they cannot all be instantly solved but most of them can be … shall we say, soothed? And just talking about it to someone you trust can help tremendously. So do not hesitate, speak to your child's paediatrician. After all, this is the person whose number you will be dialling most often in those ungodly hours from hereon.

Surfing should always be carried out with caution

Whether it is done on a surf board in an ocean or on a computer, surfing should always be carried out with caution. As far as seeking answers about parenting is concerned, many of us have overdone the internet thing at some point or the other. Yes, it is a wonderful source of as much free information as you want from the comfort of your home. It is also more discreet and less awkward sometimes, which is what makes it so attractive. Needless to say that it is certainly easier to admit to an internet chatroom filled with mothers that you stopped breastfeeding after only one month than to say it to a room full of real women.

But frankly, it is the sheer gamut of information that makes it challenging to sift out the facts from the undocumented stuff. And since the net is tremendously addictive, everyone out there has an opinion and they are anonymous, making a lot of the information even more dubious. I recall how a friend got addicted to surfing the net during her pregnancy, trying to get answers about the baby's development through the three trimesters. Despite her husband and doctor advising her otherwise, she would sit at her desk and type in a new question every morning. 'Why did my doctor ask for a second scan?' 'Is it normal not to feel the baby move for three straight hours?' 'I drank four cups of coffee yesterday. What will happen now?' And the nightmarish stories she read greatly added to her stress levels! In the end, everything turned out perfectly fine and she confessed to me later that she should have taken the internet advice with a pinch of salt and saved herself a lot of distress. So even though the internet can answer some of your questions, relying on it to give you solid, documented, dependable advice could be pushing your expectations too far. You would be much better off focusing on real people with real experiences and real answers instead.

Learn by doing

Sometimes the answers are not as objective as we'd like them to be. In fact, sometimes there is simply not any *one* correct answer. Each child is different and very often what applies to one does not apply to the other. I had heard that six months should be the perfect age to introduce solids, and mashed potatoes are the safest solid food to start with. Well, it was not to be in our case. The moment I tipped a spoonful of it into Eshan's mouth, I knew I had made a mistake. He coughed and sputtered and pretty much spat it all out within a matter of seconds! Did he hear his father complain about the high carb content in potatoes the previous day? (Kidding!) No, actually I think he simply was not ready for mashed food. In any case, I stuck to blended food for another three months. You live and you learn. (At any rate, you live …)

The power of observation

I had a colleague who used to be one of the most inattentive and detached people around, particularly when it came to things that she was not interested in. Then she became a mother and it was almost like a sensory arousal for her, as if her eyes, ears, nose et al. had suddenly awakened from a deep slumber. All at once, she was noticing everything, talking to everyone, asking a million questions all the time.

Parents are inherently observant people. (As if we have a choice, eh?) We can pick up countless tips and answer innumerable questions simply by observing what other people are doing. Like the time when my child was about four years old, there was this question that was constantly plaguing my thoughts. How do I feed him a banana? It was a simple question but no one seemed to have the correct answer. I know, I know, it was not the end of the world but when you consider the nutrition that a banana is packed with, it seemed like a pity that Eshan would not eat it. As expected, everyone offered suggestions. 'Try making a milkshake out of it.' 'Try a chocolate topping.' 'Try mashing or blending.' Nothing worked. Until the day, I saw another mum feeding her toddler one. I noticed that she did not mash, blend or top, she simply peeled the fruit and handed it over to her daughter who ate it with as much gusto as one can expect from a toddler. You see, instead of trying to distract her child or turning the banana into some uninspiring recipe or the other, she motivated the child to eat the banana by eating one herself. Every time the mum took a bite from her banana, making appreciative sounds as she did so, the little girl did the same. It worked like a charm and when I tried it with my son the next day, the result was astonishing. So, observe. It works.

Trust your intuition

Heard of that thing called 'mother's instinct', haven't you? We will discuss it in greater detail later, but suffice it to say that it often answers many questions better than anyone else can. Your baby, your instinct. Irrespective of the child's age, the kind of questions and the nature of the situation, what remains constant is the basic premise of this wonderful phenomenon. So, trust your intuition and do *not* remove that mosquito repellent patch whatever anyone else may be saying or doing. Mamma knows best.

3

'We Are Pregnant!' *Really*?

The Body after the Baby

'Think of stretch marks as pregnancy service stripes.'
—Joyce Armor

Alisha, a thirty-year-old ecstatic mother-to-be, must have been four months into her pregnancy when she and her husband got invited to a family wedding.

'Since I was well past the critical period, my husband and I chose that occasion to make the grand announcement to our extended family,' she told me. '"*We're pregnant*!" This was how my excited husband broke the news to everyone.' She smiled proudly. 'Admittedly, I was delighted with his choice of words. For me, they spelt inclusivity and equal sharing of all responsibilities. *We* were pregnant. *We* would be doing everything together. *We* would go for lamaze classes and yoga and *we* would give up coffee and wine. This was *our* baby, *our* pregnancy. *We* were in this as a couple, every step of the way.'

There *was* one thing however that Alisha's husband could not do with her, as she soon realized. That was the one thing that she had to do on her own. The one thing that was going to become her battle and hers alone—a rather long and lonely one sometimes.

However much anyone else might support you and hold you up and be there for you, you are the one who goes through all the radical physical changes that come with having a baby. And I am not just talking about the weight change or the stretch marks. The body just *feels* different and frankly, how can it not? For nine months, you were nurturing, supporting and carrying another human being inside you. If that is not something to be mighty proud of, I don't know what is. Naturally, it does help to know what to expect; after all, other than the more common changes that our bodies and minds go through, sometimes we also have to prepare to deal with some truly bizarre stuff like sudden vegetarianism; crazy, vivid dreams; different-sized breasts; sleep orgasms (that is not half-bad actually).

One mum I spoke to reported developing sudden lactose intolerance (she could no longer enjoy her morning glass of milk with her breakfast and had to shift to almond milk) while another reported the opposite. Yet, another mum shared how her feet went through massive swelling and water retention during her pregnancy. What was surprising was that the extra weight had permanently flattened the arch of her foot and she needed a half-inch larger shoe size afterwards. And to think that we always thought our shoe size was the one thing that could be relied on to stay the same. So much for that, eh?

Of course, it is not *all* physical.

'I was stressing about practically *everything* during that period, just over-thinking, over-analysing all the time,' confessed a mum friend. 'Honestly, sometimes I thought I might be going nuts!'

I think that sums it up rather well, doesn't it? The truth is that expectant mothers do not know exactly what to expect.

'A bit of a warning might have been good,' I remember telling Puneet with a sigh when my usually clear skin started breaking out like an oily tar sand, soon after I had my son. Thankfully, it was temporary, just like most of the other changes though some of it *can* take some time to settle down. And in the meanwhile, well, there is always Spanx and Perfect Magic Concealer, isn't there?

As we are well aware, there is too much pressure on women to go back to their pre-pregnancy selves as soon as they can. This also includes responsibilities at home, at work, social demands or even those unrealistic physical expectations that we set for ourselves. I don't know how many hours I have spent secretly hoping that my tummy will flatten and my face will thin out soon after popping my baby. I am sure you have too.

That reminds me of a rather funny incident that happened to me. Well, at least it seems funny *now*, at the time it felt like the end of the world. I am sure you might relate to it very well. It was a couple of weeks after Eshan was born and Puneet was treating me to a special lunch at our favourite restaurant. It was my first proper outing in weeks and I had chosen one of the dresses from my first trimester wardrobe that still fit me well (thanks to a particularly flattering stretchy fabric). It was in a deep shade of red (a colour that always looks good on me) with a ruffled belt on the side that managed to effectively conceal my tummy (or at least that was what I thought when I put it on). So, we reached the restaurant in good time and were just about to go through the security system when the lady guard there stopped me. 'Madam, pregnant women don't need to go through the security system. I'll frisk you manually.'

I stopped as if I had been shot. My baby was already two weeks old and this lady thought I was still pregnant! Mortified, I allowed her to frisk me manually while Puneet smiled at me sympathetically.

'Don't let it ruin your lunch,' he whispered to me as we entered the restaurant. 'We've come out after a long time and I want you to enjoy their popular date pancakes.'

I tried to keep up a brave face but frankly, the date pancakes were the furthest thing from my mind. I did not realize back then that I was putting an inordinate amount of pressure on myself by setting unrealistic expectations. I even made a special appointment with my doctor the next day and asked her why I had put on ten kg when my baby only weighed a little over three. Needless to say, she looked at me in surprise. 'It quite does not work like that. Post-partum weight gain is normal. It will take a while for all the extra fluids to leave your body,' she said. Didn't I understand the simplest principles of basic science? Little did she know that even the most rational women can resort to asking irrational questions when they are trying to come to terms with their new bodies and selves.

Speaking of gynaecologists, I remember reading in *Shopaholic and Baby* where Rebecca's evil gynaecologist tells her that whether she accepts it or not, pregnancy *will* slow her down? And it is true. Pregnancy has a way of getting to all of us. Yes, even those who look like they have done a fantastic job maintaining themselves, you know the ones with the seemingly incredible glow and the toned arms and legs. Don't we all know that there is more to it than meets the eye?

There is though a positive side to that as well. Considering how crazy and fast-paced our lives have generally become, it might be nice to use this opportunity to cut yourself some slack, to stop and smell the roses, as they say. And the best part is, this is one time in your life when it is okay to do just what you want, like eat that extra piece of cheesecake without guilt or take that impromptu day off from work. 'Yes, it is that moment when all your friends are dieting and exercising but you can enjoy a cupcake!'

I spoke about this to a friend who was well into her third trimester. Anjali was an advertising professional and inarguably, one of the most driven, ambitious people I knew. Her life had always been frantic, crazy, frenetic. Imagine my surprise when I went to meet her one Tuesday and found her sprawled on the couch, munching nachos and watching daytime reality television.

'I hadn't taken an impromptu day off in over four years!' she exclaimed, offering me the nachos. 'This really is a great time to kick your shoes off, put your feet up and relax. I'm going to make the most of it. My husband, by the way,' she added, 'has been very supportive.'

It cannot be overemphasized that having supportive, sensitive, thoughtful people around you can make this phase much easier. Sometimes, unfortunately, despite their best intents, family, friends, even acquaintances, can end up passing insensitive remarks and asking intrusive questions. Most of the time they do not mean to offend but new mums are sensitive and fatigued and not to be messed around with.

'You're a new mum with a lovely baby! Why aren't you beaming? Why don't you have that wonderful happy glow?'

'Because I'm going through weird hormonal changes which make my face look as flushed and red as the ripest tomatoes from the best vines of southern France. Oh, and not to mention that I cry at the drop of a hat these days. So watch it!'

So, our lives are not a cakewalk during this life-altering phase. Having said that, with the right attitude, ammunition and approach, there is a lot we can do to make the journey less arduous. Of course, every mum has her own journey, her own experiences. I do too and along the way, I have managed to pick up quite a few pointers. Some of them are more difficult and need greater effort and perseverance but some are so delightfully simple and painless that they really should be shared and passed around as much as possible. Here goes!

The first thing to do is to accept and embrace

Trust me, this is a good place to start. Whether it is the stretch marks which will fade but might not completely go away, or the belly which will tighten with time but may never be as concave as before, or even the face which will lose that puffy, exhausted look but may or may not look as sculpted as you want it to. Accept and embrace the fact that you have created a whole new human being, nourished him/her for nine months and brought him/her out into this world. That is huge! Be proud of yourself. Be *kind* to yourself. Do not beat yourself up about not fitting into those pre-pregnancy denims. These days even models and actresses (who are under so much more pressure and scrutiny) are taking a more relaxed approach to their post-partum bodies.

I recently read the interview of a popular Bollywood actress who spoke quite candidly about her own struggle. She mentioned how she overheard two people passing snide remarks about her inability to lose the baby weight fast enough. 'It hurt me for a moment and then I said to myself that it wasn't important. I have a life of my own which isn't limited to skinny jeans and a concave abdomen. I'll do things in my own time.'

Pearls of wisdom.

Set realistic goals

Setting realistic, attainable goals is better than all those grand plans we make after two glasses of wine and abandon first thing the next morning. So, set a goal that does not take everything out of you. Slot 15 minutes for a quick core workout or resolve to eat less carbs at dinner. Go for a short walk around the block and eat an apple every day. It will be a starting point and something you will feel proud of. Although we cannot deny that being a mother is, in itself, quite a workout. Just think about the number of forward bends, squats, stretches and sprints you are doing without even realizing it! Guess what is my favourite machine at the gym? The television. Kidding!

It goes without saying that those of you who are motivated enough to join that gym which does 'Mummy Motivation Mondays' or a special 'Muscled Mummies' programme, please go right ahead. You will be an inspiration to many others. Of course, it is not just about losing the extra weight though that is great too. It is also about feeling good, taking time out for yourself and doing all those super-sounding things we roll our eyes at. They work though. Also, many gyms do offer special discounts for new mums, so do not forget to ask for those. In a nutshell, set yourself a goal that you can follow through. You will find yourself gradually striving for more. Who knows one day your wee one might follow. Oh, did you know, research says that a new mum's weight loss will be noticed and appreciated much more than a regular person's? That in itself is tremendously motivating, so go right ahead and start that regimen. Hustle for that muscle, Sister!

Don't buy too many attractive post-baby clothes

Strive to get into your old ones. This was a suggestion a friend shared with me.

'Basically I didn't buy too many nice clothes after my baby was born. So other than my maternity clothes which I obviously didn't want to wear post-delivery, the only other choices were either the four collared T-shirts and yoga pants I bought after the birth or to get myself into my gorgeous pre-pregnancy wardrobe.'

She shrugged and smiled.

'I got enough motivation just looking at all those beautiful dresses and chic jeans. I ended up saving a lot of money too.'

That does not mean that you *have* to get into every piece of pre-pregnancy clothing that you own. Realistic goals, remember? Forget about the navy-blue jumpsuit which was always a bit tight. Focus instead on those gorgeous pre-pregnancy capris that used to be a little loose around the waist and could now fit you perfectly. So, this one is a winner all the way.

Try not to buy clothes without trying them on

Size 12, 14 or 16? Nope, those days are gone. You know, when we absolutely, definitely knew what size we were. Now, the task of buying clothes is no longer about straight objective numbers, in fact, it requires more subjective, careful analysis than ever before. It is about understanding your problem areas and wearing clothes that steer attention away from them. It is about focusing on clothes that fit well around the belly and preferring certain colours, more flattering fabrics and cleverer cuts. It is about going for a particular dress because the peplum design effectively conceals those trouble spots or opting for vertical patterns rather than horizontal ones for obvious reasons. And most importantly, it is about prioritizing your comfort because whatever anyone may say, when you have a baby in your arms and a pram to push as well, comfort does take precedence. Oh yes, it might also be better if you bought your clothes yourself for a while rather than have other people shop for you who do not understand your body as well as you do.

Take care of yourself

I know this one keeps popping up but new mums are so caught up with everything else that they really do need a nudge every now and then to take care of themselves. Whether that means sneaking in that power nap or booking a massage twice a month or even making an effort to look good, do take care of yourself because it will make a world of difference to your confidence and motivation. So spritz on your favourite perfume, spray a little fake tan (it gives an instant glow and does wonders to conceal stretch marks) and embrace your battle scars. They are shared by millions of mothers around the world.

4

Birthing a Father

Are Absentee Fathers a Thing of the Past?

'Dad, I have a secret. You're the best parent. Promise you won't tell Mum.'

—Anonymous

I still remember that moment. Our baby was a few weeks old. It was Puneet's turn to mind him. I had been sleeping soundly but at around 3 a.m., I stirred for a glass of water. That is when I saw it. The sweetest, most endearing sight in the world. Puneet was sitting in our old rocking chair, cradling our baby, stroking his head even as he whispered indiscernible things to him in the dark. *Baby talk*. That moment was inarguably one of the most defining moments in our relationship. He has always been a gentle-man, my husband, but at that particular instant, there was a tenderness about him that I had not ever witnessed before. Their hands were entwined and small smiles were playing on both their faces, almost as though they were sharing a beautiful secret. That was the moment when I fell in love with my husband all over again.

They say fatherhood can teach a man to be sensitive, responsible and patient. It can evoke a gentleness that even he did not know he was capable of. Despite the fact that it is the woman's body that goes through the most palpable transformation after childbirth, there is more and more evidence to suggest that the man's body goes through some remarkable changes too, including hormonal ones. Yes, you have heard me right. Researchers say that fatherhood can actually result in a drop in testosterone and a spike in oxytocin (the love hormone). There are studies which have even proved that a father's brain looks very similar to a mother's in terms of cognitive and emotional engagement after a baby is born. It seems like a pity then, doesn't it, that something that comes as instinctively to men as it does to women should have traditionally been restricted by society because of gender-defined roles? Thankfully, shifting attitudes and lifestyles have played a part in changing this as increasingly fathers come forward to share equal caregiving responsibilities while truly enjoying stepping into this amazing, life-changing role.

I remember the day one of my colleagues announced that he was going to be a father. For the sake of anonymity, I am going to call him Ashish. Now Ashish and I have worked together for many years and I have always known him to be a dependable individual, ever ready to shoulder more than his fair share of responsibility in any situation. Therefore, it should have come as no surprise to me when Ashish applied for paternity leave right before his first child was due. Yes, his wife *was* working full time too and they did not have the support of a joint family, but I think he was genuinely very, very excited about becoming a father and did not want to miss a thing. These days it is not rare to see a father who is equally, if not more, involved with his kids. It is heartening that even though his daughter is almost ten now, Ashish continues to be as involved a father as he was on the day she was born.

Have you been to a soccer field recently? No, this is not a sudden change of topic. So, if you have not been for a soccer match lately, I will tell you what to expect. My friend recently put up a post on her FB timeline. It had a short video clip of a soccer game going on and someone's voice could be heard loud and clear in the background. 'That's it, that's it! Kick the ball, kick the ball! Go champ go!' The title of the post read, 'When you can hear the dad more than the coach'.

And it is not just soccer. The same applies to ballet and music and school and doctor visits. Fathers these days are equally involved in their children's activities and palpably proud of their accomplishments. You see them everywhere, at activity classes, play dates and birthday parties. Gone are the days when a father could underestimate or be oblivious to the change a child inevitably brings to his life. The emergence of nuclear family systems, more working mums, a faster-paced life in general and changing attitudes have ensured that fathers can no longer carry on as if nothing has changed. An article on gender-defined parenting I read recently mentioned that many children born in the 1970s and '80s would remember some instance or the other of an exasperated mother, weary with household chores and child rearing, threatening, 'Wait till your father gets home!' Well, things have certainly changed around here since then, haven't they?

A father is no longer that imposing figure whose main role is restricted to disciplining the children, providing for his family and perhaps the odd ice cream treat on a Sunday evening. He is not that distant parent who returns from work in time to kiss his kids goodnight or does not know who their friends are. He is not even that bloke who waits till his child is old enough to kick a football to spend time with him/her. Today's father is a confident parent who can plait a braid for his daughter with ease, whip up a snack for his children with gusto and *even* ask relevant questions at a parent–teacher meeting. He knows how to work the bottle sterilizer as well as he knows how to drive his car. He knows which foods his children are allergic to and which anti-rash cream is best. Today's father stays awake half the night changing diapers, knows which shows his kids like to watch, is well versed with his child's social life, and is a familiar face at play groups and birthday parties.

Speaking of birthday parties, Puneet and I alternate them so that each of us can get quality time with our son and a break from parental duties as well. Not surprisingly, fathers are more likely to be around if the party is being held at a gaming or go-carting zone but that suits us just fine, right? Anyway, the heartening thing is that these days there are hardly any gender-specific zones or areas of responsibility as far as parenting is concerned. A partner in every sense of the word, dads these days very often shoulder equal responsibility with the mums, setting an example that the kids will proudly follow in the future. I am happy to say that that is the kind of father my son has.

Eshan was not yet a year old when Puneet started taking him out for father–son time. He would buckle him up in the car seat, place his bottle of milk next to his own flask of black coffee, switch on the music and they would take off. Sometimes they would go to the toyshop or a mall or a supermarket. Other times they would just go for drives while listening to Bon Jovi, Dire Straits or Michael Jackson. It is no wonder then that even today, my son's choice in music is far beyond his years and that is his dad's gift to him. Now before you start thinking that it was all fun and games all the time, it wasn't. Puneet was as hands-on at the practical stuff as I was, perhaps better than me at some things. He could swaddle, burp and feed our son like a pro. He knew the most comfortable positions to lull our baby to sleep as well as the perfect consistency to blend the baby food so our son would eat it without a fuss.

Later as our son grew older, his father knew how to comfort him at night when he could not sleep and how to distract him so he would not throw up after a difficult meal. He knew the names of all his friends, which books and authors were his favourites and which days he had martial arts or music or maths classes. Irrespective of the activity, the important thing was that they were spending quality time together, making memories that are sure to last them both a lifetime. Puneet beautifully levelled up from husband to father.

Even though I was a 1980s child myself, a time when many fathers were not as involved as they could have been in raising their children, my father, despite travelling almost 200 days in a year, made it a point to prioritise me over everything else, whenever he could. We would go on breakfast dates, he would make it a point to drop me to school whenever he was in town, we would do school projects together, he was the official games organizer at my birthday party every year (a duty he always performed with the utmost sincerity) and my go-to-man in any difficult situation. I think in a lot of ways, it was those formative years that set the base for the close relationship we share today. Needless to say, he is a very involved and loving grandfather as well, and it is indeed heart-warming to see the wonderful bond that he shares with my son.

A friend recently told me something rather interesting. We were catching up after a long time and when I asked about her family, she spoke about her husband refusing an important promotion so he could be in the same city as her and their son.

'The promotion would have meant a three times hike in salary, but it would have also required him to relocate to a different city while we stayed on in Gurgaon because of my job and our son's school,' she told me. 'Well, that just wasn't acceptable to any of us. My husband wanted to be a part of our son's life. His role in bringing up our son has been invaluable. Other than his practical contributions, our child has learnt values, real solid values, from his father. Just being around him, watching him, observing him, has taught our son things that will help him take good decisions, make correct choices and differentiate between right and wrong. He taught him to care for the environment. He taught him the importance of staying healthy and expressing his emotions. He taught him to respect women.'

The significance of this one cannot be stressed enough. Whether you have a son or a daughter, how a father behaves around women can have a life-changing impact on your child.

'It was our joint upbringing that resulted in the confident, happy, caring child we see today,' concluded my friend. 'Every child needs a role model.'

I could not agree more with that. And a father truly can be the best role model a child can have.

Another friend who got divorced when her daughter was about four years old, remembers the challenge the separation posed.

'A divorce is always difficult and traumatic for children but these days kids are even more used to having their dads around,' she confessed. 'And so, we made it a point to plan things in a way that our daughter doesn't miss out on the kind of time she enjoyed with her father before the divorce. It wasn't easy but we made it a priority. Whether it meant maintaining consistency as far as our daughter's schedule was concerned (he still made it a point to take her for tennis classes over the weekends), or spending exclusive father–daughter time on a regular basis, or the two of them going away for a vacation during the school holidays, we made a concerted effort to ensure that our child doesn't feel the repercussions of the separation. Yes, we got divorced but he's still her father. And a wonderful one at that.'

And so mums, it is time for those little pointers. These ones are extra special because they talk about what you can do to help the dad bond with his little one. Okay, I will admit it is quite a bit about what not to do as well. Here goes!

Involve him

Mum should start involving and including the dad right from the beginning and that means before the child is born. Do not let him feel left out. Do the pregnancy and baby-planning stuff together. Go to Lamaze classes with him. Go baby-shopping with him. Baby-proof the house together. Encourage him to talk to the baby. Tell stories. Sing lullabies. In a nutshell, *involve him* and encourage them to bond. Don't let him have only the bragging rights once you pop the little one.

Let them be

Yup, that really is as simple as it sounds. Unfortunately, it is not as easy to practise. Speaking for myself, the first time Puneet told me that he was taking our son for a drive all by himself, I almost fainted in shock. Our child was still so small! Yes, I do agree that he was a pretty hands-on father, but I was a new, nervous, anxious mother. Hell, even I had not taken Eshan for a drive by myself. Admittedly, a hundred nightmarish scenarios played out in my mind the entire half-hour that they were out. What if he got carsick and threw up? What if he had a meltdown? What if he missed me terribly? Okay, I know that is carrying it a bit far, particularly since it was just a *half*-hour drive but even then. Anyway, I almost fainted *again* when they finally returned, only this time it was because I was so *relieved*. While it is normal to feel anxious, stressed and over-possessive about your little one, it is important to allow the father to develop his own bond with the baby too. And that should ideally start as early as possible. So, let them be.

Accept and don't judge

No two individuals, not even spouses, have the exact same attitude and approach to parenting. I say this as much from research as from my experience. Hopefully, the parents will agree on the fundamental issues like value systems, education, health, safety and so on, but there will always be other things which you may not agree on. And that is all right. Don't judge. Whenever you disagree, remember that both of you have the child's best interest in mind. I have a colleague who was obsessed with covering her child's head with a sun hat every time they stepped out in the sun. Her husband on the other hand believed that vitamin D was good for the child and would promptly remove the hat every time *he* took the child out. In the beginning, the mum would call every half-hour to confirm that the hat was safely on. Gradually, she learnt to loosen up and accept the father's choice. Thankfully, the child too accepted that the hat would stay on when he was out with Mum, but would invariably come off when he was out with Dad.

Synchronise better

It is important to spend time as a family, all three of you, but quality one-on-one time can make a world of difference to the father's relationship with his child. Hence, coordinate your schedules and consciously slot time out. It does not just happen on its own. Puneet has always been an early bird while I like to sleep in on weekend mornings. When Eshan's social calendar began to get fuller over the weekends, we agreed that my husband would handle the morning activities and I would take over the evenings. And oh, yes, don't forget to use your free time wisely. While father and child are out watching that new ninja movie, you go to check out that new restaurant with your girlfriends. Everyone is happy.

5

To Take or Not to Take?

How to Handle Unsolicited Advice

> 'Don't let the noise of others' opinions drown your inner voice.'
>
> —Steve Jobs

As you are well aware, I was never a particularly child-friendly person. And handling my newborn was exceptionally frightening to me. You see, I had once accidentally bumped my four-week-old niece's head on the dining table in a rare moment of overenthusiasm. Thankfully, no harm was done and my cousin and her husband were very understanding about it, even insisting that I pick the baby up again but it certainly shook my confidence. Then there was the time when I locked my friend's daughter into the bathroom by mistake. I think the child's terrified screams and incessant bawling for the 10 minutes that she was locked in, must have done it. After that, I swore I would never touch a kid again.

Yet, I seemed to instantly know what to do when my own child was born. Let me explain. You remember that first night, don't you? We really did not have a clue, right? But then again, somehow we did. Yes, we read all those baby books and spoke to all those more experienced mums and even did a couple of workshops, but there was certainly something else prompting us, encouraging us, telling us what to do. We may not have instantly known how to mix a perfect formula or change a diaper or even the correct way to cradle a newborn, none of these are inborn abilities after all, but we did manage to comfort our babies when they cried and make them laugh and sleep and such. It is strange but the moment you pick that beautiful, kicking, bawling baby of yours in your arms, you seem to know exactly what to do. So what is this mysterious, almost inexplicable thing that seems to guide us, tell us what our babies need? Some people call it instinct, others like to think of it as a bond or a connection. Whatever we choose to call it, I think most of us can relate with it.

Of course, despite being a firm believer that there is indeed this amazing bond that connects us with our children, I have, like any other parent, gone through some extremely frustrating moments when nothing seemed to work. I distinctly remember this one time when my baby would cry incessantly for hours for no apparent reason. Or at least that was how it seemed to me. He wasn't hot, he wasn't cold, he wasn't hungry, he wasn't sleepy, he wasn't colicky. I recall sighing in complete exhaustion in the middle of the night and asking him, 'WHAT DO YOU WANT? I CANNOT READ YOUR MIND!' I was so tired that time that any and every kind of instinct had completely failed me. Hell, I was so exhausted that I did not even seem to have any instinct left for myself, let alone for my baby. I guess that is where observation and experience come in. Have you heard that famous quote? *No one is born a great cook. One learns by doing.* This applies even more to motherhood. I remember a popular Bollywood movie in which the girlfriend tells the ex-wife, in a fit of fury, that she wasn't born a perfect mother. She learnt by doing. That applies to all of us.

I have seen people who have had literally no prior experience with children turn into fabulous mums and dads over time. Parenting is a subjective, instinctive, intuitive, unique experience that is different for everyone and so many aspects of it can only be learnt 'on the job'. There is no one correct answer, any one perfect approach for everyone. It is something we learn as we live, something that helps us grow, along with our children. While it is wonderful to draw from others' experiences and listen to well-meaning advice and even lean on friends and family for support when we face novel situations, in the end, as they say, it is your baby. Which brings me to the bane of every mother's, in fact, every parent's existence. The problem of dealing with unsolicited advice.

'*Oh, eat what you like. Breastfeeding burns a lot of calories.*'

'*My baby's a bottle-fed one. So, I'd rather not.*'

'*Already? But it's only been a month! What does your husband have to say?*'

'*He doesn't.*'

'*Huh?*'

'*He doesn't have anything to say.*'

This conversation occurred at a business, yes *formal* business dinner, a few years ago. Thankfully, I was not one of the speakers. The one giving the advice was a fifty-five-year-old female business manager and the one at the receiving end was a youngish thirty-something project head who had only just returned to work after her maternity leave. Sometimes I wonder what it is that drives people to make personal remarks or offer unsolicited advice. We all do know that this is a condition which is more endemic to some cultures, like ours. And, this condition seems to worsen in certain specific situations: A 30+ unmarried woman, a 35+ unmarried man, a newly-wed couple planning to live separately from their in-laws, etc. But most of all, this condition seems to mutate to a whole new level when there is a new mum around. Really, when you have a new baby, suddenly everyone seems to be an authority, everyone seems to have an opinion. And it is not even limited to friends, family and casual acquaintances. I have seen complete strangers in malls, restaurants, even lifts (you would wonder where they find the time during a 30-second ride, wouldn't you) clucking sympathetically and then offering some pearl of wisdom or the other when they see a new mum struggling with her bundle of *joy*.

Could it be because a new mother looks perpetually tired, often confused, frequently uncertain and sometimes at her wits' end? From mums with older kids to the well-heeled aunties in your neighbourhood who never bothered to speak to you before, even the female boss who unapologetically refused to extend your maternity leave, everyone seems to have the time *and* the inclination when it comes to offering unsolicited baby advice. And to think that you have only *just* recovered from the barrage of pregnancy remarks and advice you were mercilessly subjected to for nine months! Just when you thought you would get a breather, starts the tirade of baby tips and suggestions. Suddenly your choices, your decisions, your *life* is open for public debate and scrutiny.

Okay, before anyone thinks I am lacking in gratitude, I am not. As a new, first-time mum, I accepted that I have never done this before and I was certainly not opposed to advice and suggestions. We know that pregnancy and babies bring out the compassionate side in most people and a majority of the advice I got was well intentioned. Sound, practical advice from any quarter is welcome. I *have* benefitted from some of that over the years. It is just that I was so overwhelmed and exhausted much of the time, it would have been great to occasionally hear what a fabulous job I was doing. And with advice pouring in from literally everywhere, it is important to sift out which pearls of wisdom to follow and what to take with a pinch of salt.

I asked some new mums to share some of the weirdest baby tips they ever got and some of them really had me laughing out loud.

'*Don't introduce fruit before veggies or he'll never eat veggies.*' (Really?)

'*Let him eat dirt if he wants. It'll help strengthen his immunity.*' (Eww!)

'*Don't hold him so much, he'll get spoilt.*' (A three-week-old baby will get spoilt!)

This might be a good time to confess that like any new mother, I have every now and then succumbed to irrational advice, as when a neighbourhood aunt told me to mix fish in my son's baby food. 'See, how smart and intelligent Bengalis are. Don't you want your baby to be brainy?' And there I was, the very next day, vigorously mixing away for all I was worth. My baby though did not care about all the labour and rejected the concoction right away.

And it can go on and on until a time comes when we simply want to turn around and tell the person, 'Give me some credit! I'm an intelligent responsible adult, I carried this child for nine months and safely brought him into the world. I *do* understand that if my child is crying, he probably needs *something*.'

Obviously, we cannot always be this candid and upfront. So how do we deal with this all-pervasive issue tactfully, sift out the useful advice from the barrage of suggestions *and* manage to preserve our sanity at the same time? Well, just like much of parenting, this one's a subjective one too. However, the following tried and tested strategies usually work.

Seek advice from parents with a similar parenting style

Puneet and I have always found it easier and more useful to discuss parenting dilemmas with parents who think like us. It is likely that we will also be more receptive to advice and suggestions from a parent who has a similar mindset. Like that time when Eshan got invited to his very first sleepover. I knew it was pointless talking to one of my closest friends about my reservations. Yes, she was a very good friend and I knew she would have my best interest in mind but our parenting styles were very different. For instance, her daughter, despite being two years younger than Eshan, had already attended countless sleepovers. She just would not have understood my misgivings and anxiety. Then I remember the time when I was trying to make an informed decision about choosing the correct school. My priority was an International Baccalaureate (IB) curriculum, solid infrastructure, a superb faculty and foolproof security. What was the use of talking to my neighbour who preferred an older school and a Central Board of Secondary Education (CBSE) curriculum, and prioritised proximity to the house over almost everything else?

Keep an open mind

Obviously you cannot follow every piece of advice that you get, you would go crazy if you did, but it does pay to keep an open mind. What this basically boils down to is that if you disregard every bit of unsolicited advice that gets hurled at you, you may well miss out on that one brilliant pointer that could save you a lot of trouble and sleepless nights. I recall this one particularly harsh winter when there was a nasty seasonal flu going around. Everyone seemed to be down with it, including my neighbour's three-year-old daughter. And that poor woman! By the end of the fourth day, she was distraught. The kid was sneezing her head off and running a high fever.

'I've tried everything,' she sighed. 'Homeopathic, allopathic, ginger-honey, steam, you name it.'

'Give her home-made chicken soup,' remarked another neighbour, matter-of-factly. 'Works like a charm, trust me.'

And it did! Not only for my neighbour, but for me as well. Seriously, that simple piece of advice has helped me and my family wade through many a difficult flu over the years. So, keep an open mind and at least listen to what is being offered. To follow or not to is always your call.

Blame it on the spouse

This one never fails. I should know since I have tried it often enough. You know that over-persuasive aunt or older neighbour whose feelings may be easily hurt? Or that school mum who is always pushing some unsolicited tip or the other on you, but whom you don't want to offend since you are going to see each other daily for the next twelve years? In tricky situations like these, you need a strategy. And what better one than to blame it on your spouse. With an apologetic smile to boot.

'The cough syrup you're suggesting sounds miraculous, but my husband's completely sold on homeopathy.'

'I'd love to drop him off for the birthday but my husband insists I stay the entire time as well. He can be a little overprotective.'

'Soccer classes are a great idea but his father's already enrolled him for swimming this year.'

Doesn't it sound perfectly sincere?

Talk to your doctor

Honestly, this one is a no-brainer. Eshan has a wonderful paediatrician who has taken care of him since he was a day old. It isn't surprising then that, from simple issues like teething pain and colic to more serious ones like a fractured collarbone at the age of four, when it comes to my child's health and safety (and plenty else), I prefer to do as the 'good doctor' says. Like the time when my son was up every night screaming with teething pain. With all due respect to frozen spoons and teething rings and chilled cucumber, a gel, which our paediatrician suggested, is what really worked for us. So much so that I made it a habit of carrying it around everywhere we went for the first few years. And oh, it is also easy to politely decline someone's unsolicited help by putting it on the doctor. It works almost every time, sometimes even as well as the spouse strategy.

'The ghee sounds great but the *doctor* recommended a nutrition supplement.'

Perfect!

Enjoy the attention

Finally, remember that a baby brings out the most helpful, most generous side of most folks. Very often people give advice simply to appear compassionate or interested. No one is really expecting us to take every casual suggestion seriously or follow it through. In fact, if no one ever offered advice and help, wouldn't you feel just a wee bit hurt and ignored? After all, you have just had a baby. Look at the positive side and bask in the attention you are suddenly getting. Soak up the concern and enjoy it while it lasts. Trust me, it will not last forever.

6

How Not to Alienate Friends And Family

Your Relationships And Other Hazards

'She never quite leaves her children at home, even when she doesn't take them along.'

—Anonymous

One afternoon, I was trying to get my baby to nap in the hope that I might be able to get some shut-eye myself. I had not slept the previous night and to add to that, it was turning out to be one of those particularly difficult days when he just would not settle down. An hour of walking back and forth with Eshan in my arms and seven lullabies later, he finally looked like he was getting ready to drift off. As his eyes started growing heavy and his eyelids began to flutter, I lowered him into the crib, sighing in relief. Suddenly, the door was flung open, and the noisy clatter of heels broke the calm of the bedroom. I turned around in dismay. Simone was standing in the doorway, smiling broadly.

'Hiya Mummy! What's up?'

'Shh!'

I put a finger to my lips but it was already too late. My baby's eyes snapped open, he looked around in panic and instantly began to bawl. For a minute, I wanted to bawl too. Cursing under my breath, I laid him on my shoulder instead.

'I'm so sorry.'

My friend started backing away with an apologetic look on her face.

'I didn't realize …'

'You never do, do you?' I could not help snapping. 'Thanks for ruining the little time I was going to get to myself.'

I suppose the fact that she was looking like a million dollars while I stood there in frumpy pyjamas and shitty hair might have added to the reaction. As for her, she was stunned to see her usually calm and pleasant best friend speak in such a nasty tone.

'I'm sorry,' I apologized, beckoning her in.

The baby was awake now anyway.

'But the thing is that you just don't understand.'

'Why do you keep saying that?' she asked me, looking hurt. 'Who understands you better than me?' She hesitated for just an instant before she added, 'Your new friends, I suppose.'

I could see she was hurting but I was too exhausted and weary to care.

'At least, they give me sound advice. You don't even know the difference between a hungry baby and a colicky one.'

'Well, I guess you'd be better off spending more time with them then.'

It was the first time we had a conversation like that. I knew that the fact that our lives and schedules were now completely different from each other had added to it. Those days, a sleeping baby was happy hour for me. I was seeing less of her and more of the mums I met in the play group or in the children's park. And when I did see her, we did not seem to be on the same page most of the time. Even as I tried not to notice the palpable hurt in her eyes, I could see something shifting in our otherwise perfect relationship. I was actually amazed I had reacted like that, it was just not like me. I could not help but wonder whether this was going to be the start of a whole 'new me' and the impact it was bound to have on my other relationships as well.

And I was not wrong. Spouse, friends, family, colleagues, every single relationship in a woman's life goes through a sea change when she becomes a mum. New motherhood is time-consuming and demanding and very often leaves little room for much else. A new mum is possessive, emotional, unreasonable, pressed for time—all at once. How can things *not* change? I found myself gravitating more towards those people who had the experience and understanding of my current situation to give me hands-on advice, solutions and support, rather than those who did not. Very often, my reactions and responses to people and situations were unexpected, astonishing, even to myself. I had a sudden alienation from my colleagues as well while I grappled with my work-from-home situation.

Hence, my reaction that day could have just been envy directed towards Simone whose life had not changed and who was still out partying until the wee hours while I was up all night changing diapers. And I am 100 per cent sure many new mums go through similar situations and feelings. Many a time, the frustration and irritation is even directed at her spouse especially when he does not understand why she cannot stay awake long enough to finish a movie or is too tired to spend the much needed couple time after dinner.

On the other hand, new motherhood can really help to strengthen and reinforce certain core relationships as well. Being a mother myself helped me understand Mum better. I became more empathetic, more understanding, more considerate towards her. I was always very close to Mum but now I found myself falling back on her in ways that I never had before, drawing on her experiences and learning from her.

As for Puneet, though we were not going out to dinner as often as before (and that is frankly quite an understatement), and not spending as much couple time together as we used to, my relationship with him went through a surprising transformation as well. Sharing the gorgeous bundle of joy brought us closer in ways that had never happened earlier. We saw a side to each other that we had not seen before. He was not just a husband any more, he was a devoted father who got home on time every evening to take our son for a drive and stayed up at night despite having to be at work on time the next day. Likewise, I was not just a wife any more, I was a mum who put all her own discomforts on one side and took delight in her child's smallest accomplishments. What we shared now was a common, deep, selfless love. He was the first person I would call every time our son did something new. In turn, he started checking on us several times a day, even dropping in for lunch when he could. Sometimes we would stay up together at night with the baby. We would nibble cookies and watch a movie and whisper like children in the dark. We would get into a squabble about which baby lotion was better for the baby's skin or whether or not he could wear shorts to the park during the monsoon. We would argue, disagree and then promptly burst into peals of laughter at the absurdity of the situation. We took decisions together, shared insecurities and fears with each other as well as joys and triumphs. It was like being in our own little world, where no one else existed and nothing else mattered.

However, it was not all peaches and cream. There were times when we strongly disagreed on issues relating to our baby and would get into ferocious fights over the most trivial things. Our disagreements and the general feeling of exhaustion that we were both going through could have easily taken a toll on us as a couple. Realizing that we now had to work harder at our own relationship as well, we started making a concerted attempt to ensure that we regularly got some couple time and consciously kept the baby talk to a limit. I clearly recall this one time when I overheard Puneet discussing his work problems with a buddy instead of with me. I could not help feeling hurt but then remembered that the last time he had tried to reach out to me, I had been too excited about Eshan's first time in the splash pool to listen to anything else. I realized that we would have to make a more conscious effort towards our equation as a couple and not just as parents. Here are a few things I started working on and which I believe, can significantly help your core relationships during this phase, whether with a spouse, your parent or your close friend.

Coordinate your schedules

I was seeing less and less of my bestie because our schedules were completely different. Simone was at work all day, I was working from home *and* taking care of a small child. Her weekends were the same as before but mine were now choc-a-bloc with play dates and birthday parties. It was challenging but the relationship was important to both of us. So one day, we jotted down our schedules on a piece of paper. On close inspection, we found a window on Friday evening. She usually finished work a little early on

Fridays and we decided that she would drop in for coffee before heading home. The timing was perfect since Eshan usually napped at that time. I made sure that I was free and the coffee was perking by the time she came around and it gave us both the one-on-one time we needed. The most important thing was that we both realized that our time spent together was sacrosanct and as much as possible, we tried not to let anything else get in the way. I am also thrilled to tell you that our weekly coffee date graduated to weekly dinner once Eshan got older and now, we girls even manage to get away for a weekend a couple of times in a year!

Try to have a proper conversation

Parenthood does something very strange to the best of us. It makes us zone out very fast. It is amazing how distracted I became after my son was born. I just could not seem to hang on to a conversation for more than a few minutes. It is the usual tiredness combined with sleep-deprivation that causes this dullness and inattentiveness. I recall umpteen situations when I fell asleep while on a phone call or dozed off in the middle of an important meeting. There were times when I don't think I could even have put half a sentence together, I was that tired. But I realized that sooner or later, I would have to start making an effort and that it was well worth it to do so.

First, having a proper, meaningful conversation is a reminder of the time when you were a thinking, intelligible human being and not just a worn-out, dazed zombie and that is always good to recall.

Secondly, after the amount of small talk we mums have to make with people we hardly know, having a real conversation with someone you care about can be very rewarding. Whether you are discussing the challenges you are facing as a new parent or even talking about something completely unrelated like an old holiday or issues you are facing at work, it is always worthwhile to pour a cup of strong coffee, sit down with a close friend or a spouse, and talk.

Keep the baby talk to a tolerable limit

Lots of parents cannot keep the baby out of a conversation for more than five minutes and very often, they do not even realize it. Sure our babies are very dear to us and we really want to talk about how sweet that first tooth looks when they smile, but perhaps your colleague or friend does not want to know every minuscule detail.

I simply must tell you about this one incident which has stayed firmly etched in my mind. I have a friend in my condominium, a single older lady from the travel industry. Let us call her Ms K. Now, Ms K and I sometimes walked together in the evening. Quite a connoisseur of food, travel and culture, she always had fascinating stories to share and I thoroughly enjoyed our walks. One balmy summer evening, I was walking with her and she was telling me all about her recent trip to Ladakh. Suddenly, I turned to her and said, 'You know, my son hasn't pooped properly since yesterday morning. Newborns usually poop after every feeding, every six hours actually, but he's been constipated lately.'

It is actually amazing how otherwise normal people suddenly lose all their social graces and think it is perfectly fine to have a conversation involving words like 'poop' and 'constipation' in a social setting, as soon as they become parents. In any case, I did not notice Ms K's bemused, mystified expression and jabbered on.

'He's on formula now so I'm wondering if that has something to do with it. Although, breastfed babies also get easily constipated. I've heard that prunes usually help with that. But I'm not sure he'll like the taste of prunes and ...'

Guess what happened next?

Ms K bade me a hurried goodbye and rushed off, almost tripping over her own feet in her hurry to get away. Now guess what she said the next day.

She messaged me saying that she was still at work and would not be able to go for a walk. Did I blame her? Hell, no! I know that ignorance is never bliss for a mum, but launching into a 15-minute monologue about my child's pooping pattern was just plain absurd. Thankfully, Ms K was understanding about it, and we did resume our walks a few days later. For my part, I made a conscious effort to keep the baby talk to a bare minimum after that and frankly, it turned out to be a welcome respite for me too. After hours of changing diapers and mixing formula, it was wonderful to speak to someone about what makes

Himalayan cuisine unique and which hotels in Lake Como have the best views.

And finally, little things go a long way

Sometimes it does not take all we have got. A new mum has a lot on her plate (mind you, there is a sharp learning curve ahead) and the people around her usually understand that it is not fair to expect everything as before. But that does not mean that we have to put our relationships completely on the side because we are parents. There are plenty of things we can do which take up no or very little time and energy, but can make the people in our lives feel loved and cared for. Puneet's favourite movie that I saved on his watch list so that he could see it later. That cup of coffee that he made me just when I was feeling down. The quick message I left on my mum's phone in the middle of a busy day to let her know I love her.

And no, it isn't *all* down to us. How our post-baby relationships pan out also largely depends on how the core people in our lives take to our new circumstances. A supportive spouse who asks you about your day and offers to take care of the baby so that you can get that much-needed break, can make a huge difference. Likewise, empathetic friends and family can be a godsend at a time like this.

On the other hand, having people around you who do not get it, can be disappointing and disheartening. In *Sex and the City*, Miranda is the first one to have a baby. She is a single working mother with very little support and understandably exhausted most of the time. To make things worse, her closest girlfriends can't seem to understand what she is going through. In fact, Samantha actually goes a step further and starts consciously avoiding her. I remember that scene when she hurriedly ushers her into a taxi just to get rid of her. Later, Miranda confesses to Carrie how hurt she is and also afraid that she is alienating her friends. She is frightened that her other relationships are all going to change, now that she is a mother. One of my close friends went through something similar. She had always been very proactive about keeping in touch with everyone but after she had her second baby, she hardly ever even managed to return any calls. As a result, most of her friends and family eventually stopped calling and reaching out to her. So much so, that by the time she was ready to return to the land of the living, she realized that she had lost touch with a lot of her old acquaintances. Thankfully, her spouse and a few close friends were supportive and understanding. Later, some of her friends confessed that they wanted to be there for her but just assumed she was busy. Many simply did not want to intrude.

Then there are those who do not have kids of their own and suddenly feel that they do not have anything in common with us any more. However, if a relationship is important, we will go the extra mile to hang on to it. Yes, we are mums now, but we are also still daughters, sisters, wives, friends and colleagues, aren't we? And oh, yes, let us not forget the wonderful new relationships and friendships we will be forging. Everyone knows that puppies and babies are like instant magnets for people. Hence, it was not surprising that I found myself surrounded with new acquaintances and friends when I became a parent. My life was no longer limited to my home, workplace and exclusive circle of friends. Now there was the park, the preschool, the mum's club, the swimming pool, even the paediatrician's office. There were so many more opportunities to meet new people and cultivate new friendships. Do allow yourself to wholeheartedly embrace these new relationships and revel in this wonderful new phase of your life.

And on that note, never ever forget the most important relationship of all. The one with yourself. You are still your own person and while it is wonderful to nurture and cherish every relationship you have been blessed with, love and cherish the one you have with yourself as well. I certainly do. Your permanent relationship status should be: Committed to growth, self-love and inner peace. Remember, you can't pour from an empty cup.

7

Travel Addict?

We Have Got You Covered

> 'Give your kids adventures, not things. Have stories to tell, not stuff to show.'
>
> —Anonymous

'You do realize that travelling is out of the question, right?'

My gynaecologist had looked matter-of-fact about it as she scribbled instructions on the prescription. As for me, the smile almost froze on my face. I guess I should have expected it given that I was already in my third trimester at that time but the Dubai Shopping Festival had already started for God's sake! Not to mention The Wine Festival in Goa and The Carnival of Venice and well, the list is pretty endless. I wasn't intending to go to *all* those places of course but the world was pulsating with energy and activity and there I was, sitting at home in my frayed maternity pyjamas!

Okay, let me explain my slightly hysterical reaction. Born with a big, brown mole on the side of my left foot, I was referred to as the official nomad of the family. Nothing gave me as much joy as seeing the sight of a packed suitcase waiting in the corner of a room, filled with the promise and anticipation of travelling the unexplored, traversing the unknown. Thankfully, Puneet shared my love for travelling and, over the years, we managed to put together quite an impressive collection of travel diaries. Those were the days when an impromptu trip to Jaipur or Agra could be organized in a matter of minutes, weekends (extended or otherwise) were always spent on the road, and two (sometimes three) proper holidays a year were a non-negotiable agreement between us. I even recall threatening Puneet with divorce when he wanted to shorten our annual summer holiday one year. Livid, he caustically asked me if those were really the grounds for divorce and I told him that indeed they were. Yes, those were the days when you would find travel magazines strewn all over our house and I had a travel bucket list as long as my arm. For me, travelling was not merely traveling. Travelling was therapy, rejuvenation, adventure and self-discovery. It was rude to leave a vacation waiting …

Hence, it was not surprising that by the time my son was three months old, I was literally going crazy. I had not packed a suitcase or boarded a flight in over six months!

'Wait a bit,' Mum advised me when I spoke to her one morning about a short holiday. 'Do you really want to rush around an airport, eat bad airline food and get jostled and pushed in a crowd, with a baby?'

'Yes! YES!' I shrieked. 'I am dying to rush around an airport and eat bad airline food and get jostled and pushed around in a crowd. As long as I get to go somewhere!'

'Well, no one said she has to go to an airport.' As always my father was trying to be the voice of reason. 'What about that wildlife sanctuary? Or that fort resort? They're both within driving distance of Gurgaon.'

'The wildlife sanctuary is too long a drive,' objected my mother. 'And that fort resort with its steep climb and rustic rooms is hardly a child-friendly place.' Child-friendly! A term I was clearly going to hear a lot in the days to come. A term that was going to become my first thought, my first question, every time I needed any information about *anything*. Is this restaurant child-friendly? Is that person child-friendly? Is that airport child-friendly? Is that *horse* child-friendly? You get the gist, right?

Anyway, back to the family conference. 'Why can't men be a little more practical? And then you go around calling *us* irrational?' Mum shook her head and looked heavenwards. 'You need to accept that things aren't the same as before. When you have a baby to think of, you can't just pack a bag and take off!'

I think that just about sums it up. When you have a baby, you really cannot pack a bag and take off. You can be as experienced a traveller, you know the kind who always has a plan and invariably ends up in the right places at the right time. You still cannot do it. It does not mean you cannot travel with babies; in fact, I firmly believe that seeing the world with your wee one can be an enormously enlightening experience. Little children have a natural sense of adventure, they love to explore, observe, discover, learn. Almost like sponges, they soak up everything and get the most out of every experience. Exploring the world with them can rekindle all our senses and allow us to see the world for what it truly is—a vast, magical, fascinating place where amazing things happen and anything is possible. Moreover, reading about a place is great, watching it on television is wonderful, but nothing, *absolutely nothing* can beat experiencing it for what it is.

Travelling is infotainment unlike any other. In a nutshell, it is the greatest gift we can give to ourselves and our children. Although, travelling with small children is a whole new ball game. New game, new rules. And the foremost rule is that you need a *lot* more careful organization and structured planning than before. Which means, you need a list. I have tried to make a broad one for you. Feel free to add what you like. We all know that there is always a lot of adding when it comes to children and lists, don't we?

Do your research and pick the place very, very carefully

I cannot emphasize this enough. It really is a nightmare getting stuck in the wrong place and that too, with a child!

Why? Because *a child is a curly, cute lunatic.* Kidding! I love kids. So first, make sure you choose a place where stuff is easily available because frankly, a place may be beautifully rustic or charmingly far-flung but if you cannot get diapers and teething gel and batteries for iPads, it is not the place for you and your baby. Then again, sometimes the seemingly best places may turn out to be the worst. This did happen to me once. It was on a trip to Dubai when Eshan was two-and-a-half. We had booked a luxury hotel which provided all the possible amenities one can think of. They even had private butlers and reliable babysitters. Imagine my shock when they categorically informed me that they would not be able to cook the instant oats that I had carried with me (the only thing my teething son ate for breakfast during that particularly difficult time) since they had a very strict food policy.

One of my colleagues also shared a similar experience. She took her three-year-old toddler and four-month-old baby on a special children's cruise. With four kiddie clubs, an exclusive children's theatre and restaurants that do daily dinner shows starring favourite kiddie characters, one would assume that the cruise would have been perfect for them, right? Smooth sailing all the way? Well, it was not to be. You see that particular cruise had a rule against allowing babies below six months. Can you imagine the poor woman's plight when they were refused entry? So do your research, ask all the relevant questions, check all the reviews you can get hold off, talk to people whose judgement you trust and pick the place carefully. And oh, get everything in writing.

Who has the time to stand around and argue about who said what when you have a baby strapped to your chest, a suitcase in one hand and a diaper bag in the other?

Pre-book everything, yes everything!

Sure your flight is booked but do not stop there. Imagine trying to convince your little one to eat pepper-crusted salmon on a flight while your neighbour's kid gets chicken nuggets and pasta just because she was smarter and pre-booked her child's meal. So be sharp about it, plan ahead and pre-book whatever you can. From things like meals on the flight, seats of your choice, hotel (you can't just land somewhere and get a *feel* of the place as before), transport to take you there, tickets for that amusement park, right down to stuff like mini–dental kits and bathrobes for the wee ones. It will make your life so much easier. We want to actually enjoy the trip and not worry, fuss or hanker over the smallest things, do we? Oh, and while we are at it, do not forget to ask for child discounts. They are available practically everywhere but very often we have to ask for them.

Pack everything you can think of

I know you might have heard the quote, 'He who would travel happily *must* travel light' but that simply does not apply to travelling with children, particularly babies. I can count a dozen things babies need daily and that is without a list! (As if packing for yourself wasn't hard enough ...) Diapers, wipes, bottle sterilizer, loads of clothes, medicines, pram, car seat, snacks, iPad, still want to go on that trip, eh? Good! You are one of the resilient ones like me. And yes, feel free to add anything else that your child may be fussy about. Each child has something special that they cannot sleep/eat/bathe without. And sometimes it takes longer to pack for your trip than the actual trip itself ...

I remember a friend who planned a weekend away with her husband and baby to a neighbouring resort. It was her first holiday with her baby and to be on the safe side, she made an elaborate list of all the things she could need. Even though they were only going for a weekend, they still managed to pack two big suitcases. As fate would have it, despite the careful planning and attention to detail, they forgot something vitally important (which invariably happens when you are travelling and even more so when there is a child). Imagine their dismay when they realized that they had forgotten the stack of Elmo DVDs without which their baby refused to eat her meals. Thankfully, since the resort was only forty minutes away, her husband was able to drive back and pick up the DVDs before the baby's next meal. Whew! Crisis averted.

Always take an electronic device with you

I recall my pre-mum stage when I would shake my head disapprovingly at exhausted-looking mums on flights and in hotels. I don't think I ever noticed the desperation on their faces as they tossed an iPad or Game Boy at their children just so they could finish their soup in peace. *An iPad for such a small child*? I would wonder. *Why can't she give him a book or a rattle*? Little did I know back then that when your own brain is rattled to the point of bemusement, a rattle simply does not work. Needless to say, I understood the significance of electronic devices almost as soon as I became a mum.

Are you shaking your head or raising your eyebrows? *I don't care*. Electronic devices have been my constant saviour thus far in my entire mum life. Anytime, *every time* that my child was about to throw something at someone or sprawl on the floor and threaten to cry until nightfall or basically do something equally appalling, it was an electronic device which came to my rescue. I know there is a lot of judgement when it comes to allowing children to use electronic devices but speaking for myself, I am done caring! Suffice it to say that a book usually cannot achieve what a tablet can. No, don't flip out. I am one of the ardent book lover types, so trust me when I say this. That does not mean that I would leave my hapless child with the little fiend for hours on end, but I do think that some particularly difficult situations could do with a bit of help. I think a long flight or a bumpy car drive or tedious train journey, basically all forms of travel would qualify. So, in a nutshell, travelling with a baby or a small child? Take something that whizzes with you. And keep it charged!

Plan for extra time

'I'm hungry *NOW*!'

'I'm not moving until I get that toy.'

'I need to pee. Yes, again!'

'I've got a stomach ache and I think I've swallowed my tooth.'

Any of this sound familiar? Yes? Great, you are probably the proud parent of a little one. I am sure you are well aware by now that travelling with a baby or small child requires a whole new level of time management. Why? (Because a young kid is like having a blender but you don't have the top for it.) A baby has a natural way of slowing you down. Unforeseen crisis situations are common, meltdowns can happen anytime and children are always hungry, thirsty, accident-prone, teary, demanding, you name it. Dozens of loo stops, snack stops, toy shop stops, play area stops, water stops, change-of-clothes stops and it is no wonder then that for the first time in your otherwise orderly and structured life, you actually missed a flight! Lesson? It might be worth your while to plan for that extra time.

There you go! That broadly covers everything, but feel free to add anything you like. And now some encouraging news for brand new parents. Babies are much easier to travel with than toddlers so make that trip NOW. After all, babies will stay where you put them since they are not mobile, and just look at the amount of time that they sleep! You'll get your pool time and your spa time and your couple time and … need I say more? So, *get out there*!

Okay, I have a confession to make. Despite the planning and the lists and the optimism, the first trip that I took with my baby was to a resort about an hour from home. Yes, yes, I do admit that that wasn't very '*get out there*' but in my defence, that particular resort was perfect for a first holiday. With acres and acres of verdant gardens where the little ones could crawl, scamper or run to their hearts' content, round-the-clock room service, babysitting services, a separate swimming pool for toddlers and last but certainly not the least, an honest-to-goodness animal farm, this was truly one of the most child-friendly places I had seen. Remember I told you that something being 'child-friendly' is pretty much a mum's criteria for most of her decisions? Suffice it to say that it was a very successful first holiday.

I suppose that first trip gave me a boost of confidence because after that, I went on a kind of mad holiday spree. No sooner had we returned from the resort than we started planning our first proper vacation to Goa. And Goa is really one of the most child-friendly (there I said it again!) places in the country. Fantastic resorts to suit every pocket, sun, sea and an overall slow-paced, languid vibe makes it a relaxing and easy destination with kids. Not to say that we were averse to happening places or anything like that. In fact, we went to Singapore the following year and we ditched the bar-hopping and spent two whole days in Universal Studios. We were actually there on New Year's

Eve! You know, when a woman tells you that she happily spent New Year's Eve in Universal Studios, you can say it with conviction that she has taken to motherhood very well. But honestly, we loved it. Then as my son grew older, our holidays grew longer. My family adores cruises and they are even better when you have a child. I would really urge all parents to try a cruise. Look at the advantages! No trudging from city to city and hotel to hotel with a truckload full of stuff. All dining and entertainment taken care of, on board. Play groups and endless activities for your little one. Seriously, it cannot get better.

In a nutshell, what I am really trying to say is that as far as travelling with your children is concerned, the opportunities are limitless and the joy boundless. It does not matter whether it is a weekend at a resort two hours away, a fortnight at a domestic hill station or seaside town, a couple of weeks in a foreign city, or a month-long summer holiday that you will remember for the rest of your life. Just plan things well, pack the baby bath tub seat (it actually does not take much room, on the contrary it creates a good barrier for other things if you place it in the centre of the suitcase and pack around it) and take off! There is really nothing that compares to the joy of watching those little eyes grow wide with wonder at the sight of something amazing and new. As they say, the greatest legacy we can leave our children is the happy memories we create together. With that in mind, get your laptop out and book your next vacation spot.

8

Being a Working Mum

How to Achieve Work–Life Balance

'Being a mother really is the highest paid job in the world since the payment is in pure love.'

—Mildred B. Vermont

I clearly remember the time I bathed my toddler with one hand, while speaking to the grocer on the phone with the other. Now add to that an urgent email that has to go out NOW and a client teleconference that I will take while at a children's birthday party, and you will understand why working mums need about ten hands like Goddess Durga!

I think most mothers would agree with me that aside from actually having the baby, this is the biggest and most difficult decision any mum has to take. When to go back to work, how to go back to work and whether or not to go back at all! Nothing simple about it and suffice it to say that we, as mothers, need to figure out what works best for us. Whether you are working from home, working from the office, working limited hours, taking a long sabbatical or choosing not to work altogether, it is *your* decision and *your* choice. Recall those famous words that Charlotte spoke in *Sex and the City*? '*I choose* my choice.' So, no judgement. Do not be harsh on yourself and certainly not on other mums. Because everyone's situation is different and most of us are trying to do our best.

As someone who started working at the age of 22, I could safely say that I had spent more time 'on the job' than anywhere else in the world. Also, mine was not a desk job. My job required me to always be on the go (client meetings, presentations, frequent trips). The result was that I was constantly in action, always out and about, which meant that my two-month-old had one restless mummy on his hands! I had technically gone back to work by then and I say '*technically*' because I was not actually driving to office. I had set up a makeshift office in our spare bedroom and was working from home instead.

Now I know that to all office-goers, working from home might sound very relaxed and leisurely with many coffee breaks and long lunches and *kanthasanchalana*s (that is a seated neck roll to relieve stress), but the truth could not be farther. Working from home is really a project in itself. A mammoth project might I add, which requires a considerable amount of planning, organizing *and* discipline.

Picture this. A WFH mum. She has finished her morning routine of feeding and bathing the baby *and* feeding and bathing herself before finally managing to settle down at her desk. The doorbell rings. The intercom rings. The cook wants to know what to make for lunch. The part-timer's husband's got some problem which strangely only *she* can solve. The laundry guy needs to be paid. The courier guy needs to be paid. You would imagine that all these things used to happen earlier as well right, the time when she was not around to take care of them. But no, suddenly it is all *her* thing. Then, as if things were not difficult enough, the internet conks off *and* the baby wakes up at the same time. No, he wants only her. You get the gist, don't you?

Now, that woman is me. By the time my unsuspecting husband would return home in the evening, I would look awful, feel awful and *was* awful to be around. I even remember watching him with envious rage each morning as he put on a business suit or sprayed cologne on his neck before he left for work. Never mind that he would spend half his day sleeping at his desk anyhow, since he was the one taking care of our son half the night if not more. I did not really think of all that because new mothers are not always very rational people. I think I finally reached the breaking point when he turned to me one day and clucked irritably. 'This coffee tastes like dishwater. You know I like it strong. You're at home now, it's the least you can do and …'

'I'm not your bloody assistant!'

I flung my napkin down and got up, pushing the dining chair away as I did. It fell over with a crash.

'And just for the record, I'm supposed to be *working* from home, not making your freakin coffee!'

That evening Puneet and I had a very civilized conversation over a glass of wine. (Don't whine have wine.) I had calmed down considerably by then and was even feeling a bit sheepish about my outburst. But one thing I was sure about. The work from home was not my scene. Again, this is a very subjective choice. While it did not work for me, it can work perfectly well for lots of women. So much depends on the kind of job it is, the kind of family structure you have, the kind of person you are. So many of my friends swear by the WFH model, as it gives them the peace of mind of being around their children and the flexibility they need during this crucial stage of life while holding on to their careers.

Since I had a dependable support system, I did manage to go back to the office. I was not doing full days and I was not travelling either, but all-in-all, the arrangement seemed to be working out. Also, despite setting certain restrictions and drawing reasonable limitations, I was doing more in less time. My productivity had increased. I was taking a shorter lunch break and fewer coffee breaks and trying to finish quickly so that I could go back home to be with my baby. However, I was not completely immune to guilt, none of us mums are. Truth be told, I am still dealing with it and my son is twelve already. Hell, there are days when he does not want me around and begs me to 'go get a life' and even then

I find myself feeling a tad guilty about leaving him when I have to. But that is just motherhood, I suppose.

Anyway, as far as making a choice about working is concerned, every woman has a different set of priorities and commitments and we all have a right to make an informed decision. Having 'been there, done that', I have tried to put a list together for all those mums who manage to successfully juggle a laptop bag in one hand and a baby bag in the other. I am sure these friendly suggestions will help you tide over those first few months when you are still trying to get acclimatized to your new 'working mum' situation. So, here goes!

Give your choice a little time

First and foremost, whatever your choice may be, give it a little time. And know that you can change your decision if you like (at the end of the day, it is *your* decision). Sometimes, we think that just because we have made a choice, we have to stick with it for the rest of our lives. That can make everything seem overwhelmingly rigid and final. It does not have to be that way. We can always decide that things are not working out the way we had expected them to, and change course. That applies to working, not working, working part-time, working flexible hours and so on. At the end of the day, working mum or stay-at-home mum, ultimately you are a mum. So be kind and accommodative to *yourself*.

Prepare for a new routine and do a trial run

If we do decide to go back to work, we have to know that it is going to involve a whole new situation and it really helps to have a timetable in place. It is not going to be easy to keep all those balls in the air but with a bit of planning and structured thinking, we can make it possible. And, whether we are depending on a family member, babysitter or day-care centre, it really helps to do a trial run. You know, it is something like a fitting for a dress you are going to wear to a big event. You want to be able to make any adjustments well in advance and avoid those nasty surprises. So do try out that morning routine before the actual schedule kicks in. Have the babysitter come over or drop your wee one to the day-care centre a day in advance and take off! This will help you figure out what really works and make changes in time. And, you can even use the free hours to go for a haircut. Bonus!

Do not start your new routine on a Monday

Getting yourself and your baby used to spending short periods away from each other can really make things easier. Allow the child to bond with the caregiver. Let them spend a couple of hours daily at the day-care centre before the real deal begins. It will help the child get adjusted faster to their new surroundings and soften the sting of separation.

And yes, try not to start your new routine at the beginning of the week. This really helps. Look at schools for instance. They usually always re-commence mid-week after the long summer holidays. Ever wondered why? Well, the first week of anything is exhausting but if you start on a Wednesday or Thursday, you will have a shorter first week to deal with and have the weekend to look forward to before you are completely worn out. That will give you the time to rest and muse over everything before you start your actual proper week.

Set expectations with your boss

Yes you are a professional and a proud one at that, but things are not the same as before. There is really no point trying to prove to yourself or to others that nothing has changed when in fact, *everything* has changed! Having a baby is life-changing and the people around you need to accept and understand that. That includes your colleagues and boss. Don't let yourself drown in work obligations that you cannot fulfil. Imagine staying up until 1 a.m. for a presentation and then waking up at 5 a.m. when your baby needs their first feed. You might do it once, maybe twice, but it cannot become a pattern. We all have got our physical limitations, and a child can really take up a lot of energy. So learn to say no, refuse what you cannot do.

I, for instance, was clear about keeping travel to a bare minimum and doing more morning–evening trips. Then again, every mum has a different set of limitations. Just make sure that you are clear about expectations right from the beginning and you do not overextend/overcommit yourself so much that it pushes you over the edge. Many mums who don't draw the line find themselves ultimately throwing in the towel and giving up their careers completely, as opposed to those who strike a healthy work–life balance.

Don't beat yourself up over trivial things

Despite your best intentions and commitment to your work, you *are* a parent now. In a nutshell, that means that your clients and colleagues will have to get used to a sudden image of a toy engine or Batman figure appearing on the screen during that webinar or videoconference. And yes, I admit that I was not always so blasé about it. Truth be told, in the beginning it used to bother me quite a bit. As a professional, I had a reputation for always being in control, always having it all together. Who would have ever imagined that I would have to sneak into bathrooms or hide behind bushes just to attend an important work call? I guess I did not want my colleagues to be witness to every little detail of my child's meltdown over a burnt chicken nugget. But you know, over time I realized that people understand. After all, we are all human. And many of us are parents too. We have all been at the receiving end of one of those not-so-perfect-working-parent moments, right? Now that we are talking about it, I have to tell you about this one time. It was a Friday afternoon and it had been quite an exhausting week. I was on the phone, coordinating my son's upcoming birthday party with Puneet. That was when a super stiff-necked client messaged me about the venue for a meeting. Pat went my reply. 'Honey, we should totally book that gaming arcade and don't forget to add chicken lollies to the menu.' It was only when I got a response a few seconds later, that I realized I had messaged the client instead of my husband. 'It's okay, my daughter loves chicken lollies too. By the way, that place is giving a 30 per cent discount on birthday parties these days.' What do you know? The client was a parent too. So you see, most people relate and understand. Go easy on yourself.

Get tech-savvy

Okay, we really cannot refute the importance of technology when it comes to anxious working mums with children at home. Whether it is a CCTV camera in strategic spots at your house (which will give some much-needed peace of mind while you are at work), or a state-of-the-art tracker device, or even a video chat every couple of hours with your little one, do whatever it takes to keep you connected. It will save you a lot of needless anxiety and at least you will not find yourself imagining the worst scenario every few minutes. New mothers are naturally wound up people with crazy hyperactive imaginations, anything and everything that can give them a bit of reassurance is worth every penny spent.

Prepare for things to go wrong sometimes

Ever heard of anything working 100 per cent right, 100 per cent of the time? Nor have I. Yes, as much as you may plan, as much as you may organize, and as much as you may fool proof, sometimes, inevitably, things will go wrong. Your caregiver *will* fall sick and usually at the most inopportune times, your child *will* act unpredictably clingy on the very day you have that critical meeting and the day-care centre *will* close for maintenance without notice. What you need in these situations is a calm approach and a reliable back-up plan. Line up alternative caregivers, look for emergency child-care centres in your area and if absolutely nothing works, simply accept it as 'one of those days'.

And finally, here's a little piece of useful trivia for all you mums, in fact, all parents who work from home. Did you know that changing out of that comfy track suit is critical to your productivity? Nor did I. So yes, even though you don't have to wear that business suit you always hated (hallelujah!), make sure you wear something crisp before you settle down in your home office. The reason is a bit psychological actually. We tend to associate comfortable clothing with sleep and leisure and certainly not with work. So, slipping into something smarter will ensure that you will have a more productive workday.

9

Super-mums Do Not Exist

Get over the Mum-guilt Syndrome

'If evolution really works, how come mothers have only two hands?'

—Milton Berle

Mums have a very unique skill. They can be amazingly attentive and caring towards others and awfully tough and hard on themselves. If you get into the mind of a mother, the one thing you are sure to find there is a barrage of questions that she is asking herself all day, every day.

Why did I give my child packaged oatmeal instead of making it at home?

Shouldn't I be breastfeeding for at least a year?

Did I ask relevant questions at the PTM?
Shouldn't my child be playing an instrument by now?
Was that movie we watched appropriate for an eight-year-old?
Should we switch to organic milk instead?

Whatever the age of the child and the individual circumstances of the mother, this is one thing we all have in common: we are constantly over-thinking and over-analysing every situation, every decision. I remember a conversation I had a couple of years ago with a friend. Her son had summer holidays going on when the Covid-19 lockdown was in full force. She was feeling bad about not being able to take him for a vacation or doing the usual holiday fun things with him. As a result, she was indulging him a bit more than usual, giving in to some unreasonable demands.

'I let him play Fortnite for three straight hours yesterday. Later, I felt terrible about it. What kind of mother allows her seven-year-old to play Fortnite for three straight hours? I should have made him do something constructive like his maths homework instead. I should have been firmer, stricter.'

'And wouldn't you have felt guilty about being too harsh on him then?' I asked her.

'I suppose I would have.' She sighed. 'We can never win, can we?'

In August 2018, a famous American sportswoman posted something on Instagram. She candidly said that the previous week had been hard, and that there were instances when she had even felt that she was not a good mum. She further stated that despite trying very hard, she constantly felt guilty about not doing enough. Her post received thousands of replies from mothers admitting they felt the same way. Famous or otherwise, if you are a mum, you have perhaps experienced this extremely common mum syndrome, also known as mum guilt. Though the dictionary does not officially list it, mum guilt does exist. It is a powerful emotion and it can be the sole driving force behind your relationships, social interactions and your career decisions. For new mums, the feeling can be even more intense. Whether it is about the time you are not spending with your kids, the food choices you are making for them, whether or not you are breastfeeding, going back to work or not, there are countless mum situations out there to make you feel like *you are simply not doing enough*.

The other day, I saw a picture of a friend from school with her three kids (God bless her!) on social media. She is a corporate lawyer who travels regularly for work. She does not live in a joint family set-up either. I stared at the picture closely. It was a holiday picture. She looked gorgeous in a short, printed dress and sunglasses, and had her arms around her kids. Her kids looked happy, calm and well cared for, and it seemed like she really had it all together like a super-mum. I quite loathe that term by the way but more on that later. Anyway, coming back to the perfect picture. Now the picture might be perfect, but life never is, is it? So they all might have posed and smiled and looked 'picture perfect' but who knows what might have happened later? For all we know, all of her kids might have had a meltdown right after it was clicked, and she ripped off her designer sunglasses and screamed like a banshee at them while the onlookers stared in mute amazement. The point I am trying to make here is that we must be very aware of the role that social media plays in adding to the pressure. Whether it is pictures of the perfect birthday parties, or your colleague's best mum moments, or even another child's accomplishments in school, social media has a way of making us feel grossly inadequate. Everyone only puts up pictures of the smiles and sunny days. No one brags about the sleepless nights, messy clothes and meltdowns. Sometimes I wish they would. It might make this whole trip a little easier and a bit more relatable for all of us.

Coming back to my intense dislike for the term super-mum. If you've watched the film, *I Don't Know How She Does It*, you will know what I am talking about. It is all there in the title. How *does* she do it? None of us can. Hence, there is no such thing as super-mum. Her myth lingers like the Tooth Fairy and Santa Claus. In fact, unlike the Tooth Fairy who has to perform her crazy duties only every once in a while and Santa Claus who has to do so even less frequently, super-mum has to perform 24x7! If that does not add to the pressure, what does?

I mean, we are all ordinary women, trying to do our best for our kids, yet messing it up sometimes. Yes, there will be take-out nights and missed PTMs and homework that is not submitted on time. There will be botch-ups at work and days when we feel that ours is the messiest house in the whole world. There will even be times when we feel that the weight of the world is resting on us. The thing to often tell ourselves is that it is okay to botch it up sometimes. It is okay to not give 100 per cent all the time. It is okay to laugh at the mess and know that the next day will be better. And no, we are not *super-mums*, thank you very much.

Now that that is sorted, let us talk a little more about mum guilt. Remember we spoke about how mums are awfully good at making lists. Well, that is where this whole guilt trip starts. When some of the things on our never-ending to-do list do not get done (and they will not be however much we may try), the guilt starts settling in. In fact, once you are a mum, it does not take long for the guilt to show up. Your baby is awake and crying for attention. You have not slept in two nights. You leave the crying baby to someone else (spouse, mum, nanny), turn over and go back to sleep. Later, *wham*! The guilt hits you like a tornado! Imagine feeling guilty about something as basic as sleeping! Or showering! Or even going to the bathroom! That is how illogical, how unreasonable this thing called mum guilt can be.

The more closely we look at the mums around us, the more we will realize that guilt means different things to different women. While one woman could feel guilty about not going back to work and leaving her spouse to be the sole breadwinner, another might feel bad about working and not being able to give her kids as much time and attention as a non-working mum. Then while one mum feels bad about being too harsh on her kids, another might feel she is taking the easy route and not being strict enough. The circumstances, the choices, the reasons are all different. The only common thing is the guilt. We are riddled with it so much of the time that sometimes it seems to consume us. It is all pervasive.

I recently read something that struck a chord with me. This lady was on a flight to Mumbai. The attendant was making her routine safety announcement. 'Secure your oxygen mask first and then assist your child,' she said in a matter-of-fact tone. 'That's when it occurred to me,' said the lady. 'Without realizing it, that flight attendant had managed to give me the most wonderful parenting advice I would ever get! If you can't breathe yourself, how on earth do you expect to assist your wee one or anyone else for that matter?'

I could not agree more. If you are on the verge of having a breakdown because of sleep deprivation or exhaustion or nerves, how do you expect to be a calm, composed mum who will take the right decisions for her child? So, it might be a good idea to stop for a few minutes and cut yourself some slack. Motherhood has become part of who you are and it certainly may be the best part, but it is not the only part. Give yourself some air, get that pedicure, meet that friend for coffee, focus on that work presentation and if you can, take that short break. I certainly did. And no, I did not go to any exotic location or anything. I did not even take a flight. I just checked into a city hotel for three nights where I could wear comfy pyjamas, order wine and pizza, lie horizontal on the bed and watch TV without being pushed, pulled or licked. Wouldn't we all like that sometimes?

And so my friends, here are some suggestions on how to deal with those fiendish feelings of guilt that seem to crop up at the drop of a hat for most mums. I hope you will be able to apply some of these suggestions to your own lives. Many of them worked well for me, so I am sure they will for you too.

Surrounding ourselves with positive, supportive people really helps

Avoid those who pull you down. Mothers work very hard, the last thing they need is to be constantly judged and assessed. That naysayer who insists on bringing up your latest parenting failure is best avoided. After a couple of times, hopefully that person will get the message. And if they do not, you have to learn to consciously ignore the unwanted remarks. On the other hand, being around people who boost you, appreciate you and give you positive feedback is always heartening. Despite all our real and imagined failures, it really helps to hear someone just tell us what a fantastic job we are doing. 'You're a good mum.'

Sometimes that is all we need to hear.

Let us not brag, compete, compare and obsess

This one is a bit difficult because parents are competitive by nature. We cannot help it. Who does not want to show off their child's brilliant abacus calculation for instance, or their little one's prowess on the soccer field? But too much competition, too much comparison will lead to a feeling of inadequacy and *guilt*. And it can start pretty early on. Forget math, and soccer, it can even be about basic stuff like who gets the first tooth first or which child begins to eat solid food first! As a matter of fact, it actually happened to me.

Eshan must have been around a year old and he had not started eating solid food. Much as I hate admitting it, this was fast threatening to become one of those things I was constantly obsessing about, even blaming myself. Was there something *I* was not doing right? I was so worried that I would seize the chance to talk to anyone who would care to listen. I actually even quizzed my gardener about it one morning. Mum could not stop laughing when I told her about it later. 'Don't worry,' she said. 'Eventually they'll all walk and talk and crawl and run. And ultimately, they'll all start eating solid food too. Why obsess over everything?'

Why indeed?

Schedule regular, exclusive quality time

If your feelings of guilt are a result of lack of time spent together, start a journal. Write down all the activities scheduled in a day. Yes, you should even put in things like brushing teeth and travel time to and from school. Then, instead of waiting for that full hour, set aside something as simple as 15 minutes together. You could listen to a song that you both like, or read a short story or maybe even just sit with your arms around your child and not do anything else. It is amazing how quality time together can be. And oh, keep the phones away. Honestly, spending time scrolling or posting on social media can eat up a massive amount of time and energy. And with people posting only their happy moments out there, the virtual world can be overwhelmingly, mercilessly competitive thus adding to your pressure and feelings of guilt. Focusing instead on real life and real relationships can be so much more rewarding. Social media is here to stay. On the other hand, your little one is growing at an alarming speed. These precious moments certainly will not be coming back so savour them while you can.

Get rid of the 'shoulds'

These '*shoulds*' are often a plethora of social expectations, family pressure and inflexible self-made rules that mums constantly impose on themselves. I *should* give my child a home-cooked meal every single day. I *should* attend every soccer game. I *should* read a bedtime story every night. Then mind you, if that was not bad enough, there are also the '*shouldn'ts*'. I *shouldn't* allow so much screen time. I *shouldn't* get home so late from work every evening. I *shouldn't* take that weekend off. Jesus! Give yourself a break and lower the bar from perfect to good enough. Good enough is good enough. Good enough works.

Finally, trust yourself

Trust yourself to take the right decisions for your kids simply because you love them. There is no one correct answer, nor any one right approach. Similarly, there is no one perfect formula for parenting. Have confidence in your own intuition, in your choices and in your decisions. No one else can have the best interest of your children at heart like you can. And that is why, whether or not your choices are the best ones for someone else, they are inarguably the best ones for your kid. So trust yourself and have faith in your abilities. They are *your* babies. You love them and where there is that kind of unconditional, total love, there really is no place for uncertainties and guilt.

10

Play Date Is No Child's Play

Mastering Play Dates And Birthday Parties

'Play is the highest form of research'.
— Albert Einstein

Eshan was about a year old when I made friends with one of my neighbours. Not that I was not friendly towards my neighbours before but once you have a child, you do tend to become more social. Anyway, I am going to call her Mrs H since her name starts with that letter. So Mrs H lived in the neighbouring tower in my condominium and she was the kind of mum I wanted to be in those days. You know, the experienced kind who always seems to know what they are doing. She had a teenaged son already you see, but her younger son was around my son's age. And so, the foundation of a brand new friendship was laid and we got into a pleasant routine of going for evening walks together, pushing our prams while we chatted animatedly about child-friendly recipes and the best playschools in the city. And all the time, I would watch and admire her, wishing I could be more like her. Now anyone might think I envied her because she knew the best way to manoeuvre her baby's pram when it got stuck in a difficult position, or because she had managed to lose *all* the extra weight within a matter of months (or at least that is how it seemed to me). But those were not the only reasons. Believe it or not, one of the primary reasons why I envied her was that she knew every single nursery rhyme under the sun! Go figure! Yes, I know, motherhood does bizarre things to us sometimes but I had never before imagined that nursery rhymes could become a cause of envy for me. Anyhow, she would sing along as we walked, and her baby *and* mine would coo and laugh as I tried valiantly to keep up. I suppose I don't need to mention that the only nursery rhyme I knew was 'Twinkle, twinkle little star'and I did not even remember all the lyrics of that one properly. Although I was singing 'Edelweiss' to my son almost every night to lull him to sleep but in all fairness, 'Edelweiss' does not qualify as a nursery rhyme. On the flipside, at least I could hope that my child's taste in music would be sophisticated.

A few weeks into our friendship, Mrs H invited me over to her house for a cup of coffee. Now this was nothing new, we usually met a couple of times a week for a coffee and a chit-chat. This time however she had some news for me.

'The lady on the fourth floor is starting a music-based playgroup,' she told me in an excited tone. 'In the condo for now, and then who knows? If it does well, she says she could expand. Did you know she has a degree in children's education from the UK?'

'That's awesome!' I was impressed. 'So, are you planning to join?' I knew she would. After all, she knew all the nursery rhymes under the sun.

'If you join with me,' she said with a smile. 'Frankly, she needs all the support she can get at this initial stage.' I stared at her for a few seconds, not knowing what to say. I mean, if you live in the same condominium, you have to show some solidarity. Then again, a playgroup and that too, a music-based one, was really not my cup of tea.

'I don't know any nursery rhyme,' I blurted out finally.

Mrs H stared at me and then burst into peals of laughter.

'So what?' she said. 'You'll learn. It's no big deal!'

But it *was* a big deal. A *huge* deal. To my own astonishment, I found myself typing 'popular nursery rhymes' in Google that very night and taking printouts of the lyrics so that I could memorise them before the big day. And there I was from that day onwards, practising 'Old MacDonald had a farm' and 'Row, row, row your boat' every spare minute that I got. (Although in my head it felt like *twinkle, twinkle little star, point me to the next bar...*) Christ, I had not practised so much even for the most critical presentations of my career. And it was not just the nursery rhymes. I had anxiety trying to figure out all the rules around this new social activity. The last thing I wanted to do was to make a bad first impression or look like a moron in front of the other mums. I wanted to look cool, calm and confident. In fact, the evening before the play date, I even spent a full hour, rifling frantically through my closet, trying to pick the perfect outfit. This was huge! It was our very first play date.

The day of the play date finally arrived. I had hardly been able to sleep the previous night but I made sure I downed three cups of black coffee before I got around to getting ready. Even though the play date was only happening in the club house of our condominium, I packed my son's bag with all the usual supplies including extra diapers, baby wipes, nasal spray, body lotion, teething gel, lactogen, et al. Who knew what I might need? I *had* to be prepared! Finally satisfied that I had everything, I slung the bag around my shoulder, slipped my feet into my brand-new, red patent pumps (big mistake!) and picked my son up. This was it. Our very first play date.

Did you know that it is very easy to separate the first-time mums from the others in a play group? And you don't even have to look for telltale signs like overstuffed baby bags or anything. You see, first-time mums are like the new students in a class. They are scared, unsure and do not know any nursery rhyme. They are also the ones who turn up for a play date in skintight jeans and four-inch patent pumps. Thank God, *thank God*, we were asked right at the beginning to remove our shoes. But that really was the only bright spot that day. By the time I had introduced myself in shaky tones to the other mothers, Eshan had already picked a fight with two other children *and* scratched a third. The mother of the boy he had scratched had given me dark looks before scooping her boy up and stomping out. Nightmare! On top of that, in my anxiety I seemed to have forgotten all the nursery rhymes I had memorised so carefully! Not that the others were experts or anything but I had never felt so mortified. I know I said that mums should not judge other mums but we all feel it at some point, don't we? Anyway, my first play date did not go well and I left the room that day, swearing that it was going to be my first and last. Little did I know that the play dates I was so dreading were well on their way to becoming my new social life. Yes, they were definitely here to stay, at least for a few years.

Now we all know that there are rules to this whole play date thing. Yup, as much as we may like to think otherwise, play dates are no child's play, at least not for us mums. Our children's social lives (and to quite an extent, ours too), depend on how well we learn to handle this. Since this is a safe space, I am going to make a confession. There was a time (not very long after the first botched up play date) when being the PPDM (Perfect Play Date Mum) was fast on its way to becoming one of my primary aims. You know the kind who always has everything under control. The kind who hands out snacks like cucumber and carrot sticks with home-made hummus (and the children actually eat them!) instead of packaged chicken nuggets and cupcakes. The kind who manages to get the children to create some fabulous piece of craft out of recyclable newspapers instead of leaving them with an unlimited supply of video games. The kind who even manages to (*gently* mind you) coax the kids into clearing up before they leave. Haven't we all seen that type, and believe me, that is the kind of PPDM I wanted to be. Now I did not exactly get there but in my quest to be one, I did manage to discover some sure-shots. And even though it took me time, once I figured them out, I never forgot them.

Don't take it too seriously

Yup, despite everything I said before, it is ultimately just a *play* date. There is no need to freak out if you are late by a few minutes or you forgot those special cookies you baked at home. Some things can go wrong. However much you try, one of the children might still throw a tantrum, or your child might refuse to eat the white-sauce pasta that he usually loves. At the end of the day, it is just a play date not a marathon. And as it is with everything else, this too shall be easier if we stay relaxed.

Always reciprocate and try to be as punctual as you humanly can

Sometimes it is nice to be invited over instead of always being the host, isn't it? The other mum probably feels the same way, so make sure you reciprocate. And when you are the one doing the drop off, try to drop and pick your child up when you say you will. This is part of common 'play-date etiquette' and cannot be stressed enough. Naturally, everyone understands unforeseen traffic jams and sudden work delays but an effort to be on time will definitely be appreciated. Plus, you will be setting a good example for the children to follow later. And oh, do offer to clean up. She was nice enough to host the play date, the least she deserves is some help in clearing that mountain of Lego bricks, play dough and KitKat wrappers in the nursery.

Always check and mention allergies

These days so many more children have food allergies than before. After all, you don't want a kid to go nuts after eating nuts. Imagine slaving over those peanut butter cookies and then discovering that the child you have invited over has a peanut allergy. Not that much fun, huh? It is important to always check about allergies (the same way we ask people their diet preferences when we invite them over for dinner) and equally important to mention if your child has any as well. And why only food, it is always good to speak to the other mum before the play date and get some background (and give some too). What kind of games the children could play, whether the other mum is cool with some screen time being allowed and so on. Your play date will go smoothly if you do that.

An ideal play date should be two hours

I read something quite interesting recently. Kids seem to magically fall apart beyond the time frame of two hours. This might be even less for younger children, perhaps an hour or so. I wish I had known about this before. I had let play dates go on for hours and was often left wondering why we had to literally tear apart a bunch of screaming, kicking, flailing toddlers. It is better to leave them wanting more, so overextending is never a good idea. And why just children? Even adults like to keep it short and sweet sometimes. Very often, I too prefer a quick lunch or coffee with a friend.

House rules should be followed

Whether it is your house or someone else's, it goes without saying that the visiting kid should follow the house rules. You may be okay with serving lunch while the kids are watching TV for instance, but many mums, like me, prefer meals to be served only at the dining table. But no finger painting with food in my house! Some mums are also very particular about the visiting kid helping in clearing up, so encourage your child to do that. Communicating the house rules if you are hosting and checking on them if you are the guest, is therefore always a good idea. And mums, support each other by urging the kids to follow the rules of the house they are visiting. Other than being the right thing to do, it will also teach the children to be considerate and thoughtful.

Should you stay?

This is a huge question. One that I am often faced with. The answer actually depends upon a number of factors. The age of the child, your relationship with the other mums and most importantly, what kind of mum *you* are. Are you the cool sort who would prefer to use the extra time to catch a quick salon appointment or a coffee with a friend? Or are you the overprotective type who balks at the idea of leaving her child in an unfamiliar place? Or somewhere in between? In a situation like this, honesty really does seem to be the best policy. If you are hosting the play date, give the mum the option of staying. If you are the visiting mum, be upfront about what you are comfortable with.

And finally, some quick pointers

These are some tips that most of us understand once we are a couple of play dates old but can still be mentioned. Don't play peacemaker for every little tiff between the kids unless things really escalate, *gently* talk to the other parent if her child is showing behaviour issues, *try* to get the kids to clean up after the date (I say *try* because it is not always as simple as it sounds), offer to bring snacks if you can, have some activities ready in case the kids get restless and most importantly, *relax*. As I said before, it is a play date not a marathon.

By the way it might be worth mentioning here that most of what applies to play dates, also applies to birthday parties. Don't get stressed is right on top of that list. I wish that was as easy as it sounds, though, considering that my son's birthday has become the single most important event in my annual social calendar—no, I am not socially starved at all—but I think most mums can relate to that. After all, birthday celebrations always go on to become some of the best childhood memories for any child and all parents want to be able to give their kid a memorable birthday that they will remember with fondness.

Of course, our birthday parties were significantly different from those of this generation. Our parties were simple albeit very enjoyable ones, usually always organized at home. No party planners or magic shows or conjurers. No theme cakes. Our birthday parties had 'finger-lickin' good' food made at home, balloons and streamers strung around the house by extended family, a game of Musical Chairs or Simon Says organized by Dad and a simple return present. Well, that is not how it is any more.

And since when did inviting the entire class become the norm? Don't get me wrong, I do it too. But then, with the number of invitees far exceeding a reasonable number (I haven't even included the parents here), how can we be expected to stay sane? Speaking of sanity, there was a time in my life when Eshan and I were attending one (sometimes two) parties every weekend and I was actually muttering words like Urban Akhada, Smaaash, Hang Out and Sky Jumper in my sleep at night. It is actually amazing how I managed to keep my weight under control but that is a different matter. Honestly, that was the time when even the mere sight of a banquet hall festooned with blue and silver balloons made me want to retch but then again, I did miss the same parties during the lockdown, which does prove that the insanity and chaos had kind of become a part of my life by then.

And here is a final tip. Well, it is really something I learnt from a friend. When you host your child's birthday, store all the repetitive, unwanted gifts in a cupboard. Then gradually pass them on over the course of the year. Considering the way birthday parties have taken over our lives, we would be spending fortunes on gifts if it were not for these genius store cupboards, right? And obviously, it goes without saying that if you have a store cupboard, you must have a list too about who gave what. After all, wouldn't it be terribly mortifying to return Misha's present to Misha on her birthday three months later?

So yes, I did manage to come a long way from that first disastrous play group. But I see my mistakes as growth spurts. In fact, no sooner did I have half a dozen play dates under my belt, than I started enjoying them. Dressed in our best clothes, we would both leave the house in great spirits and listen to music on the way. On the way back, we would chat excitedly about the outing and plan the next one. All in all, it was wonderful time spent, just being together, doing fun things, learning new skills. We attended music-based play groups, baking workshops, craft classes and themed birthday parties. We helped in organizing the annual Diwali fair at our neighbourhood club, went trick-or-treating on Halloween and carol singing on Christmas. We even joined a kids' book-reading group and movie club which quickly became our favourite thing to do on Saturday mornings. Eshan's social skills grew by leaps and bounds and as for me, along the way, I met some fabulous people, made a bunch of amazing new friends and even managed to learn a string of nursery rhymes! Sadly though, Mrs H did not stay in my condo long enough to witness my wonderful transformation, she moved away after a couple of years. Oh well, never mind.

11

Mental Health And Motherhood

How to Survive the Emotional Roller-coaster Ride

'I don't have mood swings. I have mum swings.'
—Jordan Sarah Weatherhead

One evening, I had gone down to the park with Eshan. Scores of children were running around, playing, laughing. It was a happy, joyous atmosphere and I settled down with another mum while Eshan headed off in the direction of the swings. The other lady had two children, a toddler and a three-month-old baby. Understandably, she looked a little worn out but other than that, she had quite a cheerful demeanour. We got talking and had just started chatting about the easiest way to make candy corn cobs when suddenly her toddler came running up to her.

'Mummy! Mummy!' she said, her bottom lip quivering. 'Neeya not sharing her bubble machine with me. She said she not my fwiend now. She hates me!'

And that was it! She promptly burst into tears! I am talking about the mum, not the little girl. Yup, there she was, on a public park bench, a thirty-one-year-old woman, crying inconsolably while I tried my best to calm her down (hell, we were only *just* discussing candy corn cobs, weren't we?). Her baby, taking the cue from his mother started bawling too while the toddler stared in amazement.

Bursting into tears at the slightest provocation. Weepy for no apparent reason. Overwhelmed and irritable the next moment. Staying home because you have mood poisoning ...

Yes, that describes a new mum all right. The raging hormones, stress, anxiety, sleep deprivation and exhaustion are all contributing factors. It is an entirely new world and much as we love our babies, sometimes it is almost impossible to connect with our own selves. And the physical constraints that we face particularly in the first few weeks, do not help matters. A friend I spoke to revealed that her post-delivery stitches were painful for weeks after she had had her baby. The result was that even though she was grateful for the help that she got from her family, she could not help flying into a rage every time her baby preferred to be held by someone other than her.

'It was the position,' she said. 'My stitches made it uncomfortable for me to hold my baby. I couldn't help the feelings of envy and inadequacy that seemed to take over my senses every time someone plucked my crying baby out of my arms and was able to instantly soothe him. I'd read all these wonderful stories about babies and mums instantly connecting, and seen all these pictures of peaceful, happy babies lying contentedly in a serene-looking mum's arms and really thought that was reality.'

I guess she should have just been happy about the help since it all settled down in a few days anyway. Sometimes however, it does not settle down in a few days and it is difficult to differentiate between 'baby-blues' and 'post-partum depression'. While baby blues may taper off by the end of the second week, PPD is more severe, definitely more longer-lasting and often needs professional help. However, a loving and understanding atmosphere and sensitive friends and family can make a world of difference to the new mum's mental health. The importance of helping her connect with her own feelings at a time like this and encouraging her to reach out to people she trusts, simply cannot be overstressed.

Now even though a new mum may feel alienated in these situations, as though nobody can really understand what she is going through, it is heartening to know that most other mums can relate very well with these seemingly baffling upheavals. The confounding frustration, the inexplicable anxiety, the strange dullness, the nerve-wracking confusion, it is all so much more common than we realize. There are so many of us, all in the same boat here, going through pretty much similar rhythms. And yes, even though there are professionals out there to help us deal with mood swings, emotional breakdowns or even more serious post-partum issues if they get particularly bad, nothing can beat the simple, doable and very effective tips that come from one mum to another. These are tried and tested and honestly, if we are not going to be there for each other, who is? So, let us get talking!

Bond with your baby

And no, I don't mean breastfeeding. You are not just meals on heels. I am talking about being the fun parent sometimes. Very often mums are the ones doing all the difficult, practical tasks like changing diapers, feeding and night shifts, while everyone else gets to do the fun stuff. Swap roles for a while. Delegate the practical tasks to whoever else is available and you take your baby for a drive. Listen to music. Play peekaboo. You be the one to give her that first taste of chocolate (and eat some yourself too while you are at it). And when essential chores need to be done, make them fun.

'In the art of parenting, joy is a masterpiece created with moments, not things.'– Lauren Tingley

'When my daughter was small, her bath time was late in the morning and I was the only one available at the time,' a colleague told me. 'Instead of making it seem like a chore, I made it fun. Rather than bathing her in the bathroom, I'd do it in the play pool. We'd switch on the most upbeat nursery rhymes on our music system and laugh and giggle and chat while I bathed her. Something that would have ordinarily taken ten minutes would take half an hour, but what a happy half an hour!' She smiled as she fondly recalled the memory. 'It helped me cope with feelings of dullness and stress as well. The only thing is that now she's almost ten, and still takes half an hour to bathe every morning. I suppose old habits die hard.'

We laughed but I realized that it made perfect sense. Spending happy times together is a win-win situation for both mother and child. Happy mummy, happy baby!

Get out more

The sight of a messy house and the feeling of being stuck at home can make everything seem quite dismal. Getting out more gives a feeling of positivity and normalcy. That does not always have to mean a long, leisurely day at the spa, though that is great too sometimes. When that is not possible, however, even getting out for a quick cup of coffee with a friend or taking your wee one to the playground (such a happy atmosphere too), can help. The point is to get out. And on those crazy days when nothing else is feasible, just head out for a walk around the block. Listen to the birds, smile at a stranger, play with a dog. It will give you a sense of being connected with the outside world, being a part of a larger picture, so you don't feel completely alienated.

Keep the social juices flowing

Interact, mingle, meet. I am not talking about going bar-hopping every other night of course, but keeping in touch with the people who make you happy like your spouse, family, old friends, new friends. Just connect with people other than your baby and babysitter. Take time out for some couple time with your partner and focus on each other. If you are unable to meet your friends in person as much as before, keep in touch over the phone. Don't be one of those mums who says, 'The baby's woken up. I'll call you back later' and then promptly forget to call. Call the person back. You will be amazed at how quickly people answer a new mum's call. Chat about stuff other than the baby. Make new friends at the neighbourhood park, birthday parties, kindergarten school, all the places that you frequent more. Even if you were the sort who did not bother smiling at neighbours in the elevator before, it might be worth changing that now. With limited time and a tighter schedule, neighbours are the easiest people to mingle with for quick, spontaneous get-togethers. Oh and most importantly, don't cancel plans if you can help it. That is something new mums are very good at. I think it is the sheer exhaustion that gets to us. 'Myra's had a meltdown and Mahir's spilt milk all down his shirt. I don't think I can make it.' 'I've hardly slept yesterday and my husband's just back from work. Let's do it another day.' Sound familiar? We need to change that.

Hit the gym

This one is scientifically proven. It is common knowledge that working out releases all the right hormones into your body and if anyone needs positive hormones, it is most certainly a new mum. In fact, research says that exercise has an anti-depressant effect on women with PPD. Even if you don't have the time to go to a gym or a Zumba class, there is plenty you can do from the comfort of your own home or neighbourhood. Whether it is a workout at home, or a walk around your condo, or even a swim in the neighbourhood pool, do it. Working out undoubtedly puts a spring in your step. You will look great, you will feel great! Frankly, the benefits are too many to ignore. And remember, taking care of yourself does not mean 'me first', it means 'me too'. After all, as someone wise once said, 'Your health is an investment, not an expense.'

Talk about it

Talking about it, listening to other people's similar experiences and sharing tips on how to deal with it, helps like nothing else does. Whether you join a support group (there are plenty out there that deal with just this), or you create your own, or even if you choose to speak to someone in your existing circle, it is all good. Your family must also be aware of your situation so that they are sensitive to your sudden mood changes or irrational behaviour. It is imperative that we don't feel alone or isolated because that makes it worse. Sometimes we don't even realize what we are going through and therefore, don't get the help we need. A friend or spouse or someone in your group may recognize the signs faster and recommend that you get the support you need. Remember, bad moments don't make bad mummies.

Focus on your well-being

This is the one thing that just cannot be overemphasized, particularly when we are talking about new mums. Very often a new mum is so preoccupied that she simply forgets that she is a person too. A person who needs to sleep, shower, comb her hair. A person who needs to wear a pretty dress, meet a friend, indulge in a glass of wine, have an intelligent conversation. As Katie Reed, writer and speaker, puts it, 'Self-care is giving the world the best of you instead of what's left of you.' In a nutshell, a person with normal needs. Focusing on your well-being—mental, emotional and physical—will go a long way and have a wonderful impact on your overall state of mind.

Recognize the signs

Try to learn more about the symptoms and keep a look-out for them. And please understand that it is not your fault and that it certainly does not mean that you are a bad mother. Trust me, we need to hear that often. Be mindful of what is going on, and however distressing it may seem, remember it is a temporary condition. And finally, get professional help if that is what you need. Mothers need just as much help as a newborn because they too have just been born …

12

Reclaiming Your Old Self

How Not to Lose Yourself in Motherhood

'You know your life has changed when going to the grocery store by yourself is a vacation.'

—Anonymous

As you are well aware, I was not always a particularly child-friendly person. Becoming a mum obviously changed all that but that is not the only thing that has changed drastically about me. Being a parent is one of the biggest life-altering experiences we will ever go through.

Picture this. An uncompromising, thirty-year-old, cleanliness freak with a house full of Persian rugs and European art. She wears 4-inch pointy pumps, eats sushi and sashimi with chopsticks, sleeps when she wants to, believes in travelling light, reads a book every week and listens to Andrea Bocelli.

And now, imagine this. An amenable (to almost everything) thirty-one-year-old in a house with crayon drawings on the walls and building blocks and biscuit crumbs on the floor. She wears the most comfortable floaters she can get, eats leftover pizza and chicken nuggets with her hands, sleeps whenever she *can*, carries a truckload of stuff when she travels, listens to 'Old MacDonald had a farm' and has been reading the same book for over six months. Astounding though it might seem to some, she is the same person. I call it BB and AB—before baby and after baby.

It would be unrealistic to assume that our view of the world does not change after we become parents. Some things, like time, suddenly become scarce commodities that require so much more organization. Finances need to be carefully assessed and considered before taking the smallest decisions. Other things like patience and endurance seem to increase manifold. Suddenly, everything requires planning, scheduling, preparing, organizing. Impromptu does not work, surprises are not always welcome. As parents, we need to know what happens when, where and how. For instance, we can no longer get up and run every time our friends decide they want to hit the mall like we used to. Nor can we plan vacations whenever we feel like it. Our lives now have a schedule, a structure that requires fastidious organization, almost on a day-to-day basis. I mean, we have so many more things to consider now—school, classes, bedtime, extra tuition. All that now takes precedence over everything. And switching off! What's that?

'I used to sleep until mid-morning every Sunday,' one of my neighbours confessed to me one day. 'Then I'd get up, have a leisurely cup of coffee, read the paper cover to cover and then decide where to go for brunch with my girlfriends. Now I get up at seven in time for soccer, carry my coffee in a flask to the playground and chat with the other mums while we watch our kids play.' She seemed to contemplate for a minute before she added, 'Well, at least being a mum has kind of changed me into a more disciplined person.'

Now I don't know whether being a parent makes a more patient, more disciplined person out of all of us, but what it definitely does is that it helps us realize that we did have loads of *reserves* of patience and discipline hidden somewhere deep within us which we were never aware of. Parenthood does tend to bring out the more orderly, more practical, more patient, more amenable, more agreeable, more *everything* in fact, side to most of us. It is almost like going through some sort of a spiritual awakening, a cleansing, isn't it? It is like we wake up one day and realize that there is so much more we are capable of, so much more we can fit into twenty-four hours. And frankly, if being a parent brings out the better side to our personalities, then it is a positive change, right? But does that mean that *everything* has to change? Does that mean that we have to transform our lives, our selves so much that a day comes when we can barely even recognize the people we used to be or the lives we used to lead?

'I suppose I can't completely connect with the woman I used to be before,' my neighbour concluded when I asked her whether she ever misses life as she knew it earlier. 'I remember her but can't really relate. She's still somewhere in my subconscious though because sometimes I find myself inadvertently thinking about her.' She smiled wistfully and I had to resist pointing out that she was talking about her past self as though it is another person entirely. 'It's difficult to be her though,' she remarked then, almost as though reading my thoughts. 'I realized that when the kids went for a school camp last year. It was the perfect opportunity for me to let my hair down, relax, do the things I can't otherwise. I still ended up waking up at the crack of dawn and checking my phone for messages all the time. I guess I gave up on who I used to be a long time ago.'

I know the feeling. Desperately seeking a break but not wanting to lose a single moment …

Even as I listened to her, I could not help but wonder. Is that really how it must be? Is parenthood one long hostage situation except there is nobody coming to save you?

I don't think so. Speaking for myself, yes, I now get up on the dot at six every morning and am usually asleep as soon as my head touches the pillow at night. That however does not change the fact that every once in a while, I would still like to stay awake late into the night, sipping a glass of wine while I read an exciting Mary Higgins Clark without interruption. Or the fact that even though I have slowly grown accustomed to the taste of deep-fried Mars bars and M&M cookie sandwiches with vanilla ice cream, I still like to treat myself to a crème brûlée occasionally. Yes, I am that responsible mum who can be trusted to take care of half a dozen kids in a crowded movie theatre, but I am also the same person who would like to throw caution to the wind and go parasailing or skydiving sometime in the near future. Yes, I have my schedule and my timetable typed and printed in four different places and have hourly reminders and alarms on the phone, but I am also the woman who would like to turn it all off and play the day by the ear once a week. While I take tremendous pride in my child's accomplishments and achievements whether that is his science project at school or the black belt he was awarded at tae kwon do last year, I also feel the need to do something for my own self-worth whether that is the account I bagged at work or the short story I wrote and published in a leading literary magazine. So, no, I cannot plan holidays in the spring when the weather is at its best in most parts of the world because my vacations are based on my son's school holidays, but perhaps I could think about an impromptu weekend break into the hills thrice a year. It is all about striking a balance, finding a middle path and using the opportunities when they present themselves (which they do). It is about not only embracing our new roles and lives with gusto, but also not completely letting go of the people we used to be. Yes, we are parents but that is not our only identity. And let us face it, if we completely give up on what we used to be, at some point, some little shred of regret or bitterness might rear its head, prompting us to ask ourselves the inevitable. Why couldn't you be fair to yourself? Don't let it come to that. Don't lose your identity. Don't let it be buried under diapers and onesies. It really is not that hard. It is only about allowing ourselves to give in sometimes to the little things that make us happy, letting ourselves be fun and spontaneous and human. And here is how.

Don't be afraid to say it out LOUD

I remember being at this art and craft class with Eshan when he was about three years old. Now to say that I have never been keen on art and craft would be an understatement, but I had read somewhere that art activities are great for developing a child's fine motor skills as well as problem-solving abilities and that was reason enough for me. So, the theme that particular Friday was Macaroni Art and there we were, trying to turn coloured pasta pieces into dinosaurs and necklaces, when I suddenly let out a mammoth sigh.

'Tired?' One of the other mums smiled at me sympathetically.

'No, I just miss my dim sum and daiquiri Friday evenings with my husband. They were practically a tradition before … um …um …' Suddenly realizing where I was, I stopped. Everyone was looking at me. All of them, with their blue and pink pasta strips and baby bags and glue-smeared fingers. I could not help thinking that they were probably all judging me for missing my old life.

'You know, me too!' Another mum suddenly chipped in. 'Only in my case, Fridays were always about *Sex and the*

City and Sex on the Beach. I'm talking about the cocktail of course.'

We both started laughing and one by one everyone else joined in too. The atmosphere changed and suddenly we were not only mums creating dinosaurs and necklaces out of pasta strips (though that is nice too). We were also women, individuals, with desires, hopes, aspirations and not afraid to say them out loud. Needless to say, the art classes continued but over time, the name changed from Friday Night Doodles to Friday Night Doodles and Dindori.

Take the opportunity when it presents itself

And it does. Now while the opportunity might be there, the issue is very often all about trust. You see, most mums find it difficult to trust another person with their precious little bundles. I do too. We just cannot switch off. When it comes to our babies, no one else can do what we can. Never mind that the husband is a capable, grown man who manages a successful hedge fund on his own. We are still doubtful about his abilities when it comes to Grade-2 homework and reheating noodles. Never mind that the grandmum is a mature, loving grandmother who has brought up two kids of her own very well indeed. Or even the nanny who has worked with seven other kids before and has excellent recommendations to prove it. Point? Seize the chance when it comes, hand the diaper bag to the wonderful redeemer (whoever he/she is, bless his/her soul) and take that weekend off. And please don't order 'white' pasta whatever you do. Now is your chance to pay a little visit to those crab claws with garlic butter that you used to order regularly at your favourite seafood restaurant but have not tasted in a while.

Strike a balance

All or none? Not a good idea. Instead of giving up completely, strike a balance. Find a mid-path. Obviously, there are certain sides of the 'earlier you' that just can't stick around now that you are a parent. Like the sleeping at 1 a.m. *every* single night or travelling for work without a thought to anything else. But that does not mean that you throw in the towel completely. How about more morning-evening trips or more videoconferencing? So you cannot make the movie on Saturday night because you could not find a reliable babysitter, but what is wrong with the Sunday matinee show while your child is at a birthday party? You no longer go to that fancy Lebanese restaurant because they have nothing for your child to eat, but that does not mean you are destined to spend your life at Lord of the Fries. Why not try that coffee shop that serves shawarma, has a fantastic live band *and* pizzas and a sand pit as well?

Life is all about balance and mum life is no different. Include your kids in some of your activities as well. Take them when you go grocery shopping. Let them accompany you to the mall and help you choose the perfect pair of shoes. Alternate the music in the car. It will help them to understand early on that their mum is an individual in her own right with desires and aspirations of her own. Not only will this be wonderfully rewarding for you, it will also do the kids a world of good and make them into selfless, accepting, accommodating, generous human beings. Balance is the base for any healthy, happy relationship—the one with your child is not different.

13

Mum Friends, Your New Best Friends

How to Build a Support System of Friends

'Ain't no party like a mum friend party because a mum-friend party ends by 8.'

—Anonymous

When I had my son, I had a good, healthy circle of friends. However, at that time I firmly believed that as far as friends go, quality reigns supreme. Those were the days when I could literally count my friends (I am not considering casual acquaintances here) on the fingertips of one hand. Now twelve years into motherhood, I can safely say that I can strike up a conversation with anybody as long as she is a mum. Yup! That is right. She may be tall or short, working or non-working, Indian or Japanese, master chef mum or fashionista mum, as long as she is a mum, I can talk to her. Not to say that I am the quintessential socially hyperactive mum, you can always spot those out in a room within seconds. They are usually the ones to initiate all the WhatsApp groups and social plans and their kids always get invited to every single birthday party or play date. Nor do I have an instant connection with every mum I meet. It is just that despite all the differences in the whole wide world, two mums will usually find *something* to talk about. We may have completely different lives, completely diverse personalities, but there will still be enough common ground for us to bond over.

For all of you who are familiar with the girls from *Sex and the City*, you might remember the time Miranda had a baby. Okay, okay, I know that I am about to quote them again, but there was a phase in my life when I used to watch the series *every* single night. So, Miranda is a single mother and a lawyer to boot. Translation? She is exhausted all the time. One particularly bad night, she is almost ready to throw herself off the fire escape when her neighbour comes to her rescue.

'Don't any of your girlfriends have babies?' she quizzes her and Miranda shakes her head.

'But they've been very supportive,' she clarifies.

'No, believe me, if they don't have children, *they don't have a clue*,' states her neighbour emphatically.

And that is the gospel truth, my friends. And that is why mum friends are the indispensable support system to every new mum's survival and sanity.

Mum friends are the people who know exactly what to say when you are distraught because your child refuses to eat, they are the ones who will understand if you take three days to get back to a simple text, they are the ones with crayon drawings and school timetables proudly stuck on the walls of their newly decorated living rooms. Very often mum friends live close by, making popovers and impromptu help convenient. They *get* you and most of the time, they have your back. They are going to be your new best friends and even though you will not know it in the beginning, many of these friendships will last you a lifetime. The bonds and relationships you form during this very remarkable phase, will always hold a special place in your life. Today Eshan is twelve years old but close to 70 per cent of my closest friends are the women I met during my initial years as a mum. Like the instant friendship I struck up with a mum at his preschool. I had never met her before in my life, but we felt like kindred spirits right away! How could we not? Not only were we both new mums, we were the *only* mums who would hang around the empty school, long after everyone else had left, anxiously looking out for our wee ones. A couple of weeks later, we felt confident enough to leave the kids in the safe confines of the school and step out for a quick coffee together. How far we have come from that first coffee. Today, I can easily say that she is one of my closest friends.

As far as social life and getting out is concerned, the first year of motherhood can pose some challenges. A new mum leaving the house even for a simple chore requires the planning akin to a NASA launch. That sums it up, doesn't it? Then, on top of that, a new mum is usually cranky, forgetful and exhausted. That is partly because of sleep deprivation and crazy physical demands. I mean, try opening a stubborn high chair with one hand all the while juggling a wailing baby and a plate of baby cereal with the other. All on three hours of sleep! And even though our colleagues, friends and even our families say they understand, *do they really*?

'All my friends were carrying on with their lives and jobs like before—working, socializing, having fun—while I was struggling with my new role and job as a mother!' said Priyanka, an interior decorator who took a sabbatical from work after she had her first child. 'It could get isolating sometimes.' She sighed. 'I can't tell you the number of times during those initial months that I would be desperate to get out of the house for a while, even just for a simple cup of coffee. But I had to take my baby everywhere I went. I know my friends would have tried but they wouldn't have really understood. They'd have wanted to go to some completely unsuitable, sophisticated restaurant where the waiter doesn't bring you crayons before the water and the menu doesn't have French fries.' Priyanka rolled her eyes. 'Honestly, I couldn't even have imagined life without French fries back then.'

I tend to agree with her since I went through something similar. Barely a couple of months into parenthood, Puneet and I got invited to a colleague's house for dinner. Now this colleague is a single woman and lives in one of those very grown-up apartments where you simply can't imagine taking a child. Think expensive porcelain and crystal everywhere and sushi and tempura for dinner. Since Eshan was two months old, I did not want to leave him for three straight hours, so I took him along. How did the evening go? Suffice it to say that it was not that much fun. Not for my colleague, not for my son and definitely not for us.

Changing your whole life is never easy and the only people who really seem to get you at that time are other mums going through exactly the same thing. It would not be an exaggeration to say that my mum friends turned out to be a true blessing during those initial years. With similar schedules and circumstances, making plans and doing things together was effortless. We filled in for each other, cheered and backed each other's choices and decisions, held each other up when something went wrong, and even exchanged notes on how best to sit through an entire animated film with a bucket of caramel popcorn or a plate of cheesy nachos. The kids were happy, we were happy, it was a total win-win. Sometimes we would meet at home, other times we would take our kids out to child-friendly places where the children could play and we could have a natter over a peaceful cup of coffee.

Speaking of child-friendly places, I particularly remember this farm which hosted a Petting Day for children on Sundays. It was a wonderful place. There were tame farm animals the children could interact with, acres for the kids to run around in, wholesome home-cooked food and lots of sunshine. Really, if you are a new mum, find yourself a farm. You can't go wrong with a farm.

Not to say that making mum friends is as easy as all that. On the contrary, it can be downright hard sometimes. Some women might create divisions in a group, be openly judgemental and aggressively competitive. Also, not everyone finds it easy to mingle with new people. For instance, I know a lady who is a self-confessed introvert. It is understandable that she finds it exhausting to make small talk with people she barely knows. 'Small talk is my nemesis. How can I be friends with someone when the only thing we have in common is that our children go to the same tennis class?' she said to her husband one evening. She had a point but most mums find themselves dragged into the social scene once their children are old enough to understand social interaction. If you have a curious, interactive child who loves to mingle and enjoys being around other children, you just have to make the effort. Studies show that being with other kids has a very positive impact on a child's overall development. It teaches them skills like sharing, boundaries, empathy and problem solving. So, making an effort is worth it. That does not mean that you have to be a social butterfly or be best friends with all the mothers of the kids your child is friends with, but perhaps you can find a middle path. You can have a perfectly cordial, pleasant relationship with most of the mums in the group you meet at the playground, and who knows? You might meet a few like-minded women you can really get along with, and a few who might even become your closest friends and turn into unwavering pillars of support for you.

Here are a few tips for mums who find it hard to develop new friendships. They are brief, swift and bang on!

Try more one-on-one play dates

One-on-one play dates are better for bonding and not every outing has to be with an entire army. One-on-one play dates give more opportunity to spend quality time and really get to know what a person is like. For instance, that lady you meet at the school gate every morning might look like a very warm and interesting person, but how would you ever know if you only meet her at birthday parties amidst the din of video games and dozens of other chattering mums? Invite her over for a one-on-one play date one Saturday afternoon. Talk about travel, books, movies, while the children play peacefully in the next room. You might realize to your delight and amazement that you have more in common with her than you could have ever imagined.

Don't set your expectations too high

Be realistic and accept that you do not know most of these women very well. Rome was not built in a day and neither is a new relationship. If you are still *feeling* your way around a new friendship, don't make crazy overambitious plans that last through the day. 'I met this lady at my daughter's tennis class,' confessed a friend to me once. 'When we realized that both of us were planning to take our kids for the same Disney movie that weekend, we decided to go for the movie together followed by lunch and then a play area.' She sighed. 'It was only at lunch that we discovered that while I was an ardent animal rights activist, she was a celebrated member of one of the oldest hunting clubs of India. I guess we should have said goodbye after the movie…' So, your initial meetings with other mums should be like first dates. Keep the timing short and don't let yourself get overwhelmed. Keep it brief and if you click, it will give you something to talk about the next time you meet. And if you don't gel, well, you are not stuck there forever.

Find like-minded mums

Having more in common than just your children will make interaction much easier and more interesting. If you are a bookworm, find a Mum and Me book club in your city. If you are a sports enthusiast, go to your child's soccer classes. If you are passionate about the environment, join a climate youth organization with your child. You will be there with your kid, you will meet other like-minded parents *and* you will manage to have a good time too.

You don't have to socialize every time your child does

Learn to delegate. Delegation always works. Get your husband, best friend or nanny to take your child to some social events too. While we all want to be there for our kids, we don't have to be *everywhere, everytime*! Stay home, have that glass of wine and binge watch a show. After all, how many times can you sing 'Old MacDonald had a farm'? Right? Right!

Meet your mum friends in 'non-mum' surroundings too

Try to meet your new friend for a movie (needless to say, a non-Disney one) while the kids are in school or go for a drink to a local pub. It is always fun to bond over a Tequila Sunrise or Cosmopolitan, isn't it? Let your hair down together, laugh, have a good time. Your mum friend is not only a mum, she is also a woman just *like you*. Meeting her outside the 'mum-environment' will give you a fresh perspective on her personality and you will be able to appreciate her for what she is—an interesting individual with hobbies, interests and opinions.

Take time out to meet your 'other' friends too

That is the term I am using for all those non-mum friends. They are as vital as mum friends. You see, motherhood can really take over your existence. There is an entire world where I am primarily known as Eshan's mum. That can be overwhelming and we all need a break from that.

There are times when you do not want to talk about Julia Donaldson and open house and broccoli. You will want to be reminded of a time when you were not a mum, forget about homework and timetables and carpool, and not talk about your children at all. AT ALL.

While we are on the subject of mum friends, have you thought about the term 'dad friends'? Now I don't really know whether or not that term actually exists, but I firmly believe that it should. If women can bond over teething issues, homework and junior league, why not men? What is sauce for the goose is sauce for the gander, isn't it? Speaking from my own experience, I know my husband can safely say that today several of his close friends are other fathers he had met at birthday parties and school events and in the park. Just like mums, dads are able to relate better with other dads too. Sometimes much as one might want to, it may be difficult to meet that single friend who is free to go pubbing every Friday night, since he obviously does not have to take his child for a 7 a.m. sports class the next morning. And your husband might realize that he has more in common with the other dad he sees twice a week at tae kwon do classes than he initially thought. He meets him frequently, they share the same misgivings and fears and they can relate better with each other due to the simple fact that they are in similar phases of their lives. It is therefore not uncommon to see two fathers planning a play date, or taking their kids for a picnic or going bowling together. It is like a win-win-*win* situation. The kids are happy, dads are happy, *you* are happy.

In fact, did you know that these days there are actually apps which can help dads find and connect with other like-minded dads? They are like communities aimed at supporting dads and soon-to-be dads, and frankly, it is not a new trend at all. Remember that endearing scene in the movie, *What to Expect When You're Expecting*? You know the one when the 'dudes' enter. Well, they are actually a group of normal dads, they just call themselves 'the dudes'. They meet at a local park every Saturday, complete with prams and slings and diaper bags. They consider themselves a sort of 'fight club for dads' and they have got their rules. No judgement (this one is the most paramount), unquestioned loyalty and confidence (what goes on in the playground stays in the playground) and unconditional support for each other are the ground rules. They are open-minded, understanding and very welcoming when accommodating a new member. Sounds good, doesn't it? Most importantly, they made fatherhood look cool all those years ago and I can't agree more with the film's message that dads should bond with other dads for camaraderie, companionship and support. Well, the movie is more than a decade old and that just goes to show that dad friends have actually existed longer than we know. So, what is your child's dad waiting for? Get him to form his own group of 'dudes'. Believe me, they will be a treasure trove of support, encouragement and comfort.

14

Master of One or Jack of All Trades?

How Not to Let Your Child Succumb to the Rat Race

'[N]othing is fun until you're good at it.'

—Amy Chua

Eshan had just celebrated his fourth birthday when I decided to start scouting about piano classes for him. No, I don't sing or play an instrument myself but then our times were different, less competitive. As a mum who wanted the very best for her child, I could not help noticing that most of the four-year-olds I knew had already started attending some music class or the other.

'Music helps them with coordination which is really important at this stage,' one of my mum friends told me one day. 'It also helps them manage their time and attention.'

She then proceeded to show me a couple of YouTube videos of children as little as three years old playing Mozart on the piano. I guess seeing those little prodigies made quite an impact on me because I began my search the very next day. However, it did not take me long to discover that making a choice was not going to be easy because quite frankly, our city seemed to be crammed full with options. There were keyboard classes, guitar lessons, flute classes, vocals, drums. The choices were plentiful, all we had to do was choose.

Admittedly, I was partial to the piano, I have always felt that it is particularly elegant. After checking out several teachers who could come home to teach, group classes and even professional schools, I came across a school in DLF Phase 1. One sunny Sunday morning, I went there with my mum friends and our children. We were then given a full tour of the school including their classrooms and practice rooms which were complete with grand pianos, good enough for a professional concert. The fact that the children's hands were still too tiny to fit properly on the full-sized keyboards, did not really seem like a deterrent at that time. We were too impressed with their world-class infrastructure and faculty to consider anything else. Totally sold on the idea, I registered my child for a three-month programme. Little did I know then, that even though we had joined the basic, elementary programme, there was nothing elementary about it at all. On the contrary, within a matter of a few days we realized that it was downright confounding! I mean, imagine a four-year-old sitting on that wooden bench, his legs not quite reaching the floor, his hands too small to be properly placed on five adjacent white keys together. Even though he has still not learnt to read a simple book independently, he is expected to make sense of the fact that a weird-looking symbol on a sheet represents a key on the piano and that is just one of the dozen instructions that he is expected to follow, all at the same time! And the homework! Let us just say that for a hobby class, it did seem like a lot. In any case, he was too little to do it on his own and that is when I realized that I was expected to help him. I tried to explain to his teacher that I was quite clueless as far as playing a piano was concerned, but I don't think she understood my predicament. 'How can she expect me to help with this homework?' I grumbled to Puneet one evening. 'I don't know anything about this stuff.'

'You're a parent,' he laughed then. 'You're supposed to know everything about *everything*.'

How right he was! As parents, we *are* expected to be experts at everything. Speaking for myself, despite my initial protests about the piano homework, I did assist my son in whatever limited capacity I could. I did not want him to fall behind everyone else and so I gave it my best shot, struggling with worksheets that were frankly quite indiscernible to me. But that was just one example. Suffice it to say that if you are a parent, you should be able to make an origami bird, sing a Spanish song and understand an American sport. You should also be adept at knowing how to troubleshoot an iPad, bandage a sports injury and host a Halloween party.

Fortunately, kids these days are better able to cope with all this and more. Christ, these days they are even doing coding classes and designing their own websites at the age of six! Children these days are smart, they learn fast and they are innately competitive. I remember the time we visited New York a few years ago. Now the The Metropolitan Museum of Art is a must-do on every tourist's list but I was in two minds whether to take my son. He was just eight at the time and even the guards there tend to look dubiously at anyone below 4ft 6in. They are responsible for guarding billions of dollars' worth of art, after all! Anyway, no sooner had we entered the museum, than we were in for the surprise of our lives. Not only could Eshan positively identify and interpret world-famous art, he seemed to understand the reverence with which it needed to be treated. 'That's *The Starry Night* by Vincent Van Gogh,' he announced with a decisive nod, leaving everyone in the vicinity open-mouthed in amazement. And he even pronounced 'Gogh' the way it is supposed to be pronounced. As for me, I could not stop staring at him. All that the name Vincent had meant to *me* at the age of eight, was that it was the name of my father's friend from Goa who sent us the most delicious plum cake every Christmas.

It is no wonder then that parents these days find it difficult to keep up with their children. Nor is it surprising that this general competitive environment does make us feel grossly inadequate at times. Our children have been looking up to us since they were babies, relying on us for solutions and answers. It is not easy to shake your head and admit to your child, 'Sweetie, I'm sorry, I don't know this.' That is the thing though. Admitting it should not be difficult. At the end of the day, it is important that our children understand that their parents too are normal, regular human beings with limitations and imperfections. It also happens to be the right example to set for our young ones. Yes, we want them to be ambitious and goal-oriented, but do we really want them to turn into over-competitive, aggressive individuals who drive themselves beyond their own endurance? I don't think so. We would much rather like them to be committed and focused on what they choose to do and appreciative of their own accomplishments as well as those of others.

Let us talk about simple ways to work around this so that all of us can manage to set healthy examples for our little ones as well as successfully preserve our sanity.

Engage with your child's learning but enlist help when you can get it

Some things need to be reiterated. Much as we would like to be, we really *can't* be experts at everything. So enlist help when you can get it. If there is someone in your family who is good at a particular subject, request them to help out.

My dad, for instance, is a maths whizz. Result? Eshan gets straight A's in maths despite the fact that I still get occasional nightmares about my maths exams. Furthermore, if your child needs extra help somewhere, get him that extra tuition. Leave the sports coaching to the coach and the guitar lessons to the music teacher. Make a deal with that neighbour who happens to be awesome at art. If she can help your child with drawing and painting twice a week, you could help her kids with their reading. That way, everybody's life becomes easy and you get to spend more quality time with your children, doing the things that you genuinely enjoy.

Don't raise the bar so high that your child starts feeling pressured

The activity schedule of an average child has increased in leaps and bounds over the years. What has not increased however is the length of the day. A day is still twenty-four hours long and with so much more crammed into it, it is no wonder that most children feel pressured and stressed to perform. Not to mention that a relentlessly frenetic schedule leaves no room for relaxed fun time with friends and family. Really, I see children these days and I sigh in exhaustion.

Let us take the example of Eshan and his friend who shifted to Singapore. Both boys promised each other that they would stay in touch. True to their word, they both created Skype accounts and promised to touch base once a week for half an hour. Not a big deal, right? Wrong! It was only when we tried to coordinate their schedules that we realized that it was not going to be easy. One boy had chess lessons every Tuesday and Thursday followed by soccer practice. The other boy had maths classes every Monday, Wednesday and Friday and tae kwon do on the weekends. Both had birthday parties to attend practically every weekend, book clubs and debate groups, apart from their regular schoolwork. As for us mothers, we were just shocked that slotting out a mere *half-hour* once a week was proving to be a challenge. So stop and take a breather. Figure out what the priorities are and keep the expectations reasonable.

A little perspective helps

Yes, our kids are being exposed to everything and it is all very easily available these days with speciality classes and institutes literally *springing* up all around us. In fact, the options are quite limitless with swimming, tennis and soccer being offered in most condos, art and music in the neighbourhood, coding classes online and so on. That certainly does not mean that children have to work at making *careers* out of them all! Each child is different. Discover what your child is interested in and steer them that way. A little perspective always helps. I identified three things that Eshan really enjoyed doing and encouraged him to focus on them. Frankly, I would much prefer him to be master of one rather than jack of all trades. And if you are going to master one thing, you are going to need focus, commitment and perspective.

And finally, please, please do not fall prey to stereotypes

When I think about the number of months I spent trying to coax Eshan to take a keener interest in cricket though it was clear that it was just not something he enjoyed, I wish I could rewind back to that time and do things differently. Can't say that I completely blame myself though. After all, cricket is practically a religion in India! The pressure got to me, I guess, just as it does to most parents. How can it not? It is relentless.

'Every child must play a sport. Sport teaches teamwork.'

'Coding is a basic literacy in the digital age.'

'Cricket is an essential game. It's hugely popular.'

'Art is a cultural awakening for children.'

'Playing an instrument teaches them patience. And it's calming.'

Calming? *Calming*! Nothing about all this sounded calming to me. It sounded like an aggressive, manic, never-ending race, and frankly, I don't think anyone gets to the finish line.

15

Inculcating the Habit of Reading in Your Child

How to Give Your Child a Headstart in Life

> 'Children are made readers on the laps of their parents.'
>
> —Emilie Buchwald

Eshan was just about seven months old when I started reading to him. The result was that he developed a love for books very early, a love that grew as he did and I think that is one of the greatest gifts I could have given him. A voracious reader and a keen writer myself, I would have been extremely saddened if my child had no interest in reading. Being an only child in a time when a single child in India was unusual if not rare, I know that one can never feel lonely if one has a book in one's hands. Books can take you on the most incredible, most fascinating journeys of your life, can give you the most remarkable experiences you can ever hope to have. 'If you're going to binge, literature is definitely the way to do it.' Oprah Winfrey could not have been more right! I wanted that for Eshan, so I took a decision to start him off young. Obviously, we were not reading proper books at that time, just some basic sound and picture books to pique his interest, but it was still a wonderful thing to do together. Reading together makes for the most amazing bonding time with our children and can give us truly heart-warming memories. And that is why I decided to dedicate a separate chapter to this.

Now before I became a mum, I never really noticed the children's section in a bookshop. You know how it is. What doesn't concern you, well, it doesn't concern you. I was a complete novice at children's reading with absolutely no knowledge of things like reading level, attention span and language skills. I had no understanding of how to pick age-appropriate books that would spark an instant interest in kids. It was not surprising then that the first time I went looking for books for Eshan, it was like discovering a fascinating new world. There were activity books for all age groups, recipe books for kids, encyclopaedias, biographies of famous people, books on superheroes, sports-related books. And the story books! Ooh la la!

It was like stepping back in time, into the magical world of *The Enchanted Wood, The Wishing-Chair* series and *Charlie and the Chocolate Factory*. I asked the owner of the shop if he had books for children under one and nodding enthusiastically, he led me to the brightest, most colourful part of the shop. *The Very Hungry Caterpillar, Sea Friends, The Big Book of Dinosaurs, Where's Spot?, Peter Rabbit, Winnie the Pooh*—all beautifully arranged on floor-to-ceiling, wooden bookshelves. Eagerly, I stepped forward. What followed was a very happy half an hour that I spent, literally surrounded by rows and rows of the cutest sound and picture books you can imagine. I think I might have even got a *little* carried away (books do that to me sometimes), but I was smiling from ear to ear by the time I managed to stagger back to my car with my loot. And there was no looking back after that.

We settled down into a bedtime routine the very next day. It is said that the best time to read with your child is just before they go to bed, and I agree. Not only does it make for wonderful bonding time with your child, reading also has a very calming and soothing effect on the mind which is exactly what your child needs to go to sleep. However, there is no hard and fast rule. You can read with your child whenever both of you can make time in your schedule. Just try to allocate a reading space in your child's room and settle down together. A good way to start is by reading aloud to your child and the more animated your reading is, the more interested the child will be. Reading aloud helps to strengthen vocabulary and pronunciation, and also helps younger kids to imagine and visualize. You can even take turns to read out loud which will make the kids feel more involved. Now with younger children, while you may be the one reading out loud, do get your child to participate by holding the book or turning the pages. Slowly but surely, bit by bit, the bedtime reading will become a habit, a part of daily life that your child will get hooked on to. It certainly happened with us. So much so, that Eshan even insists on carrying a couple of books with him when we travel. And oh, one very important tip. Do try to pick up a phonic and vocabulary library if you can. Every child should have one. It was what ultimately taught my little one to read independently. Anyway, even though Eshan is twelve now and is reading Sherlock Holmes and Greek and Roman myths, we have still got some of his earlier books which we did not have the heart to give away. We have kept them as mementoes and we have no qualms in admitting that every once in a while, we cuddle up together and flick through one of his special baby books. It brings back the most wonderful memories for both of us, and for me, I get my little boy back, even if just for a while. But the most important thing is that I have managed to achieve what I had set myself out to do. I have made a reader out of him and quite an avid one at that. Thankfully, young readers these days have plenty to choose from, with so many more shops dedicating bigger sections to children's books and more options available online as well. The focus on children's reading is steadfastly growing with read-aloud workshops and book clubs for kids and even interactive online sessions with their favourite authors that our little bookworms can revel in. All we parents have to do is ensure that despite the intrusion of digitization, we don't let our kids miss out on the simple joy of reading books. 'All children are born readers,' my mother said to me once. 'It's the parents who can steer them either way.' I could not agree more. Here are some tips that I would like to share with the parents of young readers. They worked for us and I hope they do for you too.

It does not matter what your child is reading, as long as they are reading

I remember overhearing a school librarian talking to a young, worried mother one day. The lady had been trying to coax her daughter to read more but the little girl was just not interested in reading.

'What does she like? What fascinates her?' asked the librarian with a confident smile. 'Dinosaurs,' the lady replied.

The librarian promptly pulled out *The Big Book of Dinosaurs* from one of the wooden shelves. It had a glossy, colourful cover with a gorgeous, larger-than-life image of a dinosaur on it.

'This should be good to get her started,' she said to the lady who gratefully took the book and thanked her.

The librarian told me that the mum returned a week later with her daughter in tow. The girl was hooked! So in a nutshell, it does not matter if your seven-year-old is not reading Roald Dahl or Enid Blyton. If the child is interested in soccer, get him *The Everything Kids' Soccer*

Book. If she's interested in world leaders, get her Nelson Mandela's or Abraham Lincoln's abridged biography. The important thing is to get them reading. And as long as the reading is informative, age-appropriate and relevant, it is all good. As J. K. Rowling rightly said, 'If you don't like to read, you haven't found the right book.'

Start a book-swapping or exchange programme

Children's books are not cheap, especially books for very young kids. Most of those are hard-bound and glossy and many of them have pop-ups, sound and 3D effects. Furthermore, you will end up giving most of those books away as your children outgrow them and you need to find place for newer books. So even though you want your child to read as much as possible, it is just not practical to buy every book out there. I always found it very disheartening when I refused Eshan a book. On the one hand, I was encouraging him to read and on the other, I was denying him the very same thing. Thankfully, a friend came up with quite a brainwave. She started a book-swapping/exchange programme with a few of her child's friends. Suddenly, the options were limitless! I daresay that the little ones were thrilled and we even started coordinating our purchases so that there was no repetition. After a few weeks, we extended the book-swapping programme to include a book club as well where the children would meet once a month and discuss the books they were reading. The one thing to remember however, is that the book-exchange programme can only work if the children have similar reading levels. But it is certainly a practical and economical way to go, if you want your child to read as much as possible during those early formative years.

Get your child a phonic and vocabulary library

I know I said this before but some things have to be stressed. A phonic library is a beautifully structured set of books with all the phonemes in a tried and tested order of progression, starting with simple letter sounds to complex and variable spelling and pronunciation. Not only does it teach your child to read independently, it also helps in building confidence. It was our phonic and vocabulary library that made our 'Learning to Read' journey so much easier. In fact, right after we had completed all fifty books in our set, my son expressed the desire to start reading on his own. That was one proud day for me.

Make reading time sacrosanct

Today, Eshan cannot conceive of going to bed unless he has done his reading. Parties, social events, extra homework—nothing comes in the way of our reading time. Obviously it is not always an hour, sometimes it could even be as less as 15 minutes, but it is very definitely there.

Reading, like everything else, should be free of gender bias

To cut a long story short, if your daughter cannot connect with Nancy Drew and wants to read Hardy Boys instead, she should, by all means. Similarly, your son might discover that he really enjoys reading about the escapades of the O'Sullivan Twins, and does not really care for the latest soccer book. Avoid gender stereotyping and bias when it comes to reading.

Buy more books as birthday presents

How many times have we all received or given presents which are either not appreciated or just not useful? Speaking for myself, I tend to buy a lot of books as birthday presents, Christmas presents and even return presents because I read somewhere that books will occupy a special place in your child's heart and mind if you create an association with special days and events. On his fifth birthday, Eshan received a personalized book called *Lost My Name* as a birthday present. It takes the child on a magical reading journey with alphabets and the answer at the end of it, is the child's name. I still remember how thrilled and wonderstruck my son looked when he turned the last page and saw his name there in bold, glittery lettering. That is what books can do to a child. So, think 'books' every time you need to pick up a present for someone, particularly for a child because they will truly be treasured for a long time to come.

Get involved in your child's reading programme at school

Most schools have a reading programme these days. I remember the day I saw the junior library in Eshan's school for the very first time. To say I was ecstatic would be an understatement. It was one of the most beautiful junior libraries I had seen, complete with an enormous reading tree. You could get anything from a leaf to a bud to a flower on the tree, depending on the number of books you read. The biggest honour is a crowned owl and I saw children as young as four years old, striving to be on top of that tree. The winners would be rewarded with a pizza or an ice cream or a pyjama party at the end of term with their pictures taken and displayed on the school's page on social media. It is immensely motivating for the children and I am delighted to share that hardly a term has ever gone by when Eshan has not been a crowned owl on that tree. It is one of those accomplishments that he always takes a lot of pride in. And do you know what the best thing is? In the beginning, hardly 25 per cent of the class used to make it to the tree but now more than 50 per cent are up there! That is why I agree with that statement, 'All children can be readers, we just need to encourage and motivate them.'

Let your children pick the books themselves

A new nationwide study that surveyed children between six and seventeen, shows that children clearly prefer to read books that they pick out for themselves rather than those that other people might choose for them. So let your child pick the books themselves and don't stop them if they want to reread a particular book. We have all done that, haven't we?

And so, my friend, reading is the best gift you can give to your child. Whether you are reading to your child or reading with him, there is always something very special about curling up together with a good book and a cup of hot chocolate. Disappear into a world of magic together, go on those wonderful adventures, share those remarkable experiences with each other and make memories that will truly last a lifetime. As they say, 'Reading is a passport to countless adventures.' Who would not want to give their children that?

16

Choosing the Right Preschool

How to Ensure Your Child's Smooth Entry into the Real World

'Teaching preschoolers is a walk in the park. If that park is Jurassic Park.'

—Anonymous

Over the years, I have observed that children are naturally inquisitive. They are like sponges, eager to learn, ready to soak up as much information as they can. Having said that, there is no perfect age to start your child on a structured learning programme. I am not talking about proper school here, that usually starts at a standard age of four. I am talking more about a preschool or even a pre-preschool, like a play group or a 'Mum and Me' programme in the neighbourhood. In general, children in India start preschool earlier than their counterparts in the West, but it all depends on how quickly you want your child to start adapting to life outside of their homes, how much social interaction you want them to have and what your general circumstances are. In fact, these days there seem to be educational programmes for children as young as two years. Again, you don't *have* to opt for one of those, it all depends on your outlook and your situation. I remember this lady who contacted me right before my son turned two. She was marketing a set of educational books for very small children. The books were the interactive sort and came complete with a smart pen which meant that they were, um … quite expensive. Add to that the fact that the content *did* seem a wee much for such small kids (I thought a detailed world atlas for a not-yet-two-year-old was taking things too far.) After much deliberation, I finally decided not to buy the books. I had also put off checking out preschools in my city, at least for a while (unlike some of the other mums I knew). As far as I was concerned, there was no hurry at all. I knew that the jury was still out on the perfect age to start kids on a structured learning programme, but in general I felt that very small kids greatly benefit from being in the safe and nurturing atmosphere of their homes, around the people who love them.

I waited for Eshan to turn two before I started looking at preschools in my neighbourhood. That task, though, proved far from simple. Quite a novice in this particular area, I had heard that school admissions could prove to be a real nightmare, but I had not realized that it included preschools as well. I guess I fully understood the seriousness of the situation only when a friend told me about a much sought-after preschool in my city where you need to go on a wait list even before you have actually had the baby!

That certainly got me thinking. Add to that the fact that your child is still so tiny (just looking at them can make the idea of preschool seem frightening), and you can be sure that choosing a preschool qualifies as a Herculean task. Truth be told, there are a multitude of factors that need to be considered when choosing a preschool. Practical factors like the distance from your house, safety factors like the kind of security they provide, hygiene factors like whether they have sanitizers in every classroom or not, are just the tip of the iceberg. Adequate research must be done, elaborate tours must be taken and references must be sought out. And that, my friends, is how it all starts.

The first school that my son went to was just a thrice-a-week 'Mum-and-Me' learning programme. However, because it was a part of the early learning programme in one of Gurugram's biggest schools, I had high expectations from it. I have to confess that my grandmother was pretty appalled that a child who was still in diapers was being taken to school and I am sure many of you would have had similar experiences with older people in the house. That just goes to show how much everything has changed over time.

Anyhow, our first day arrived sooner than we had expected, and trust me when I say that I was incredibly nervous and excited, all at once. My son was going to school! Admittedly, my excitement had fizzled out a little by the time we finally reached it after a tediously long and bumpy ride. And the building! It was huge! The distance from the main gate to the side entrance for primary children must have been at least a kilometre. Add to that an unwieldy pram, a fussing baby and a needlessly unhelpful guard, and I had no idea how on earth I was going to get my son to class on time. On his first day too! And let me tell you at the outset that the rest of the morning did not go very well either. I was exhausted after walking in the scorching sun for ten minutes with a load of baby stuff, my son was miserable and the classroom disappointing. Eshan was still on baby cereal so could not eat the eleven o'clock snack that was served, most of the kids were cranky that morning for some reason, and all in all, the interaction seemed to be more about managing a bunch of bawling kids rather than any sort of learning. We returned home three hours later, discouraged and disillusioned. I was already dreading going back. And even though I did stick it out for a couple of weeks more, we gave up soon after that. Perhaps, it was too soon.

Our second experience as far as schools was concerned was very different from the first. This was a preschool too but somehow, for a number of reasons, it was smooth sailing from start to finish. Perhaps the shorter distance and smaller, cosier and more comfortable set-up made a difference as did the fact that my child was six months older. He spent almost two years there and other than the first couple of weeks (which is a very reasonable adjustment period), I cannot think of a single hitch. Our experience was so positive there that it actually gave us the confidence we needed to start proper school later. I still remember how wonderful the teachers were and what a fantastic events calendar they had. There are many beautiful memories from that preschool that I think will always remain firmly etched in my mind. His first sports day, his first school diary (it was a gorgeous pale blue colour with little stars all over it), Diwali and Christmas celebrations in school, Grandparents' Day (I recall how my father's eyes had glistened when Eshan proudly took him for a tour around *his* school). Then there was the first role play, take-and-talk activities every week, his first picnic and the very first PTM (I was truly very impressed with how professionally they conducted it). In fact, I quite literally had tears of joy in my eyes when my baby graduated from there (they had the most adorable graduation ceremony, complete with a graduation gown and cap). Basically, it goes to show that taking the correct decision about the preschool can make all the difference to our peace of mind as well as to our children's well-being. Because what a teacher writes on the blackboard of life cannot be erased. Here are some basics that parents might want to think about when taking a decision about a child's preschool.

Don't skip the preschool

It is called preschool for a reason and it really can act as a wonderful stepping stone to proper school later. The hours at preschools are limited, the systems more flexible and the atmosphere more home-like. All in all, it is a friendlier and easier environment in which to get your child familiarized and acclimatized with the concept of going to school. And, other than playing a major role in getting the little one prepared for the outside world, going to preschool also enhances learning, thus giving the children an edge when they finally start proper school.

Consider the distance

I know this might sound old-fashioned but it is not. It is practical advice from a mother who has driven for an hour each way on bumpy roads with a bawling two-year-old. Sigh! I feel weary just thinking about it. Also, we must never forget that sudden, unforeseen emergencies are normal with small children and you want a school that you can dash to within minutes. Add to that the fact that a typical school day always starts early and you have got your answer. I mean, would you want your tiny, exhausted child to spend an hour each way to and from school? Of course not. So, consider the distance and opt for a preschool which is conveniently located.

Bad hygiene has to be a deal-breaker

Preschoolers' immunity is not strong yet, hence they are prone to falling ill more easily than older children. Plus, schools are hotbeds of infections and cross-infections (children are constantly either biting, licking or kissing each other) and small children can be dreadful carriers. Believe me, there were actually several infections and illnesses that I had never even heard of until I became a mother. Hand-foot-and-mouth disease for instance. Sounds uncomfortable, doesn't it? And so, a school which has the promising sight of hand sanitizers placed in strategic locations, clean and healthy looking staff, and hygienically prepared meals being served to kids, has to be on top of your list.

Safety and security is of paramount importance

Are the ID cards of parents/caregivers checked thoroughly before children are handed over at dispersal time? Are there enough security guards stationed? Are there sufficient security cameras to monitor the comings and goings of people? Is the school child-friendly in the way of staircases and elevators and so on? These are the questions parents should ask when taking a decision on a preschool for their little ones. And check as many times as you want. Don't hesitate. Your precious little bundle of joy is going to be spending three hours a day, five times a week here! So, go right ahead and ask away! And take an informed, safe decision. In this case, it really does pay to be a little extra vigilant.

The teachers and staff

Do the school staff look friendly and approachable? Does it seem like they care? This is so important. At that age, we are looking to give our kids a loving and nurturing atmosphere. So even though it is great to have a teacher with an impressive degree in children's education and superb knowledge of her subjects, what such small children need in order to really blossom and bloom is some tender, loving care. And quite frankly, preschoolers are not easy to manage. Very often preschool teachers really do have to double up as mums/dads/grandparents and what not? It is no wonder then is it, that patience is a quality that all preschool teachers must have in plenty, particularly if you consider how physically exhausting the job can be? Actually, I have always thought of it more as a vocation than just a job. Because teachers who love teaching, teach children to love learning. Thankfully, we were lucky as far as preschool teachers were concerned. I particularly remember Mrs Basu, Eshan's first official teacher. She was tall and gentle with snow-white hair and a grandmotherly look about her. I must say she could be strict and firm when she wanted and stood no nonsense from anyone, but there was still something very compassionate about her and all the children seemed to instantly take to her. She was particularly instrumental in helping my child adjust to school in those initial days.

And so, my friends, make the best of those beautiful preschool years. They are special in a way nothing else is. The tantrums, the tears, the triumphs, the trophies—it will all combine to give our children the wonderful start that they need to step into the world. You will find your eyes brimming every time those little feet hesitate to step into class on those hard days, your heart overflowing each time those tiny hands bring home a cookie that was saved from snack time especially for you, and your lips saying a prayer of gratitude every time your little one comes home from school bursting with all the wonderful things that happened that day. A mix of myriad emotions and experiences, those preschool years will always be remembered with fondness, since so many special 'firsts' in your child's life will happen there—the first uniform, the first friends, the first teachers, the first poem, the first race. So make sure you hold on to it as best you can because really, the preschool years seem to fly past at an unbelievable pace and then before we know it, our children are ready to make their first steps into the world.

17

Settling Down in Your Second Home—Your Child's School

How to Hone the School–Parent Partnership

'Together may we give our children the roots to grow and the wings to fly.'

—Anonymous

Did you think you were done with the 'waking-up-at-the-crack-of-dawn' phase of your life when you graduated from school? Well, that is not how it works. Far from it. You see, you are a parent now. Don't worry though because you are not alone. Speaking for myself, I swear the 'waking up early' part was the biggest bummer of my entire school life and the sole reason I heaved a sigh of relief on the day of my school graduation. Obviously, I did not think about the fact that that phase would make a comeback one day for at least another twelve years or so. The only difference being that this time *I* was the parent and thus, I would be getting up even earlier, in time to get my wee lad to school punctually.

So now that your child has graduated from preschool, it is time for those little feet to enter the real world. If you thought that finding the right preschool required perseverance and dedication, brace yourself. Finding the right *big* school (as it is commonly referred to), is several times more challenging. In fact, this is the one time when doctors, lawyers, corporate professionals, homemakers, artists, writers et al. will come forward solely as mothers and fathers, and jostle for a frontal space in the same line. The line for school admission forms.

As though things were not hard enough already, school admissions in our country are a complete nightmare. For a new parent, it can be quite a daunting experience. The sheer numbers are responsible for that, as they are for most of our grievances. Anyhow, first things first. Get your research done. Trust me when I say that the research is quite an uphill task and by the way, I am a research professional. I suppose it might have something to do with the enormity of the situation. This decision is going to have a life-changing impact on our children and we certainly don't want to blunder here, do we?

Once the initial research is done, we do a deeper dive. We start talking to people. We talk to everyone. And everyone has an opinion, particularly when it comes to schools. Then lists will be carefully, meticulously drawn up, pros and cons will be marked and discussed with the spouse, the family, the friends (actually anyone who will care to discuss them), till you can discuss them no more. Strangely, the lists will be promptly torn up, only to be made again. Can you begin to see the detailing, the analysis, the intense scrutiny that goes into this? Suffice it to say that hereupon, every single mealtime conversation, every single day, will be on the same subject, and anxious parents will lie awake for hours, night after night, wondering, pondering, considering. Then school visits will be scheduled (if the schools are kind enough to entertain us in the first place). Subsequently, second visits will be scheduled (or rather second visits will be humbly requested), forms will be procured, painstakingly filled up and submitted. And then the wait shall start. The wait for some good fairy to sprinkle some magic dust on us, so that we might have the good fortune of getting a call from one of the schools of our choice. Once the calls start coming in, another list will be prepared, analysed and discussed. And finally, finally, the fees will be paid. Whew! No, double whew!! And a brand new chapter starts.

When we think about it, twelve years seem like a lot but most parents will agree that a child's school life seems to pass by in a flash. Speaking for myself, I actually cannot believe that my son is already a seventh grader. It seems like yesterday when I was dropping him off for the first time, anxious and sceptical about how his first day would go. Honestly, I can never forget those initial days. I used to spend a good part of the morning in the school waiting area (in case my child had a meltdown or something), with the lady at the reception giving me exasperated looks every now and then. Thankfully, I was never alone; there were always a few other overanxious, nervous parents like me. Anyway, even when I used to eventually return to my office, I would have my phone on the highest ring tone all day, lest I miss a call from school. After all, schools these days have much longer hours and a kindergartener always seems so tiny. I swear I cried like a baby the first time I went to pick him up after a full day. It was the first time he had been away from home for eight long hours and I still remember how tiny he had seemed at that enormous school gate, clutching at his teacher's hand and looking out anxiously for me. How far we have come from that.

Today when I see him bounding into school each morning, excited and happy, I am so glad that we put all that thought into choosing a school for him. As they say, those twelve years that the child spends in school will undoubtedly be *the* most defining years. He will learn things that will shape the coming years of his life and what he chooses to do with them, he will cement relationships, bonds and friendships like no others, and he will realize his own potential, worth and place in the world. It is no wonder then that school is considered a second home. Here are a few things that are worth thinking about and can contribute tremendously to a healthy and fruitful school–parent relationship. You might want to include them in your thought process too.

The noteworthy nine

According to experts, there are nine minutes in a child's day that are most important. It is said that a child's emotional health can depend hugely on how we interact with them and guide them during these key moments. They are the three minutes after the child wakes up, the three minutes after they return from school and the three minutes right before they go to bed. These are the moments that undoubtedly need a parent's keen involvement and participation.

In fact, the three minutes after a child returns from school can be the most unpredictable. Since every day in school is different, a child's mood is different every day. Sometimes, they may rush up to you, almost falling over in excitement because something they did has been appreciated and praised in class. Sometimes they might beam at you happily and tell you all about the new student who has invited them for their birthday party at that cool new place in town. Other times, they could be quiet, withdrawn and sullen and it might take all of your convincing ability to get it out of them that they have had a fight with their best friend and they are not speaking to each other any more. Make yourself available to your child and focus on what they say. Try to share in their joys and triumphs, offer them comfort during moments of distress and encourage them when they are feeling disheartened. You will get a deeper insight into the mind of your child, and it will keep you involved as well. So, do make a note of the noteworthy nine!

School is your second home

Speaking of involvement, remember I had mentioned earlier that school is like a second home? Well, I was not just talking about the children. I was talking about us parents as well. So much so that whenever anyone talks to me about my son's school, I always refer to it as 'our school'. And why ever not? I mean, this is the one place that is going to be constant in your life for the next twelve years. Its number will hold the position of supreme importance in the contact list of your phone. The one place you will know like the back of your hand. The parents you will meet in your child's school are the people you will see most often, the people who will soon go on to become your new best friends. Your schedule and even your vacations will largely depend on the school's timetable and calendar. PTMs, annual days and open houses will be sacred dates marked into your calendar weeks in advance and nothing, absolutely nothing, aside from a natural disaster will prevent you from keeping those commitments. That is how much a part of your life the school will be.

Parent involvement: How much is too much?

When Eshan started school, we knew that our role would not be restricted to dropping and picking him up daily. We *wanted* to be involved. Having said that, I knew I was not the type of mother who would spend hours over the weekend laboriously making props for a school play, or even the kind who would dutifully volunteer for every single school trip. Don't get me wrong, I really admire parents who do that, but that is just not me. And I know that my son would agree with me. I remember the time when I had to visit his school three times in a row for something. By the third day, he had enough. 'Are you coming to my school *again* today, Mum?' he asked me exasperatedly. 'Don't you have somewhere else to go?'

So then, how much is too much?

That depends on what you consider too much. In all honesty, there is also a practical side to this. At the end of the day, however much you may want to volunteer in the school activities, you have to see how much time you have on your hands *and* how interested you are in a particular activity. For me, any commitment that I make to my son's school is sacrosanct, which is why I am always careful about making only those promises that I am very sure of keeping. That might mean taking up a stall for the winter carnival every year (it happens once a year and so, that is not too difficult), or sending in a word of gratitude every now and then (I firmly believe that teachers and educators are instrumental in shaping the lives of our children and need to be appreciated more often), and most importantly, reinforcing and supporting the learning that is happening in school.

A friend who is head of the department for sociology with one of Gurugram's leading schools always says that parent involvement in school life gives the children a clear edge. And it is true that when parents and teachers work together towards a common goal, it leads to reinforcement of behaviour, skills and even values, and children experience much better self-esteem, motivation and success. The importance of that just cannot be stressed enough.

The school diary and class blog

Since we are on the subject of involvement and participation, we all know that these days schools do not entertain frequent telephone calls from parents, don't we? And rightly so! Imagine the plight of a single teacher trying to ward off queries from scores of parents, some of them very anxious ones. Admittedly, I am one of the anxious ones. In fact, in several schools, parents don't even have access to a teacher's telephone number after a certain grade. How then can parents stay involved with their child's life in school? Enter the school diary and class blog. The diary particularly, is the main thread of communication between the parent and the teacher. Important announcements, issues or problems pertaining to the child's behaviour, accomplishments which need to be appreciated or celebrated, as well as important events which need to be marked in the parent calendar, are all noted down in the class diary. I for one never miss checking the diary since I learnt my lesson the hard way, a few years ago. It was the *one and only* time I missed reading the diary and as luck would have it, there was a Show and Tell the next day. I had to run around like a headless chicken at seven the next morning looking for an oversized red T-shirt and a floppy hat that would fit Eshan's head! Trust me, it might sound funny right now, but it was a complete disaster when it happened. Lesson? Always check the school diary.

Then there is the class blog. This one is almost like taking a peek into your child's typical day at school. I clearly remember the time when Eshan was in nursery and food seemed to be every parent's primary concern. Is my child eating properly or not? That question really seemed to dominate every discussion, every interaction with the form tutor. The class blog was such a comfort during that phase since it gave us a glimpse into the time that our children were spending in school. We could sit back and enjoy candid pictures of them in the dining hall, in the soccer field, in the library, in the dance or art class, participating, studying, laughing, eating, looking well, looking *happy*. Every parent's dream come true!

Homework and learning

Homework assignments are another thing which deserves special mention. Things have certainly changed in that area from the time we went to school. Don't we all remember how we carried tons of homework back every single day and our school bags sometimes weighed almost as much as we did? It was not surprising then that we felt more like beasts of burden than schoolchildren, lugging those satchels back and forth! Did you know that there has been a revolution of sorts since then in the laws pertaining to school bags? The government did actually pass a law in November 2019 announcing new rules limiting the weight of school bags. Anyway, coming back to school assignments, most schools nowadays do not believe in giving tons of homework daily. Nevertheless, there is always something or the other that needs to be done. The good news is that schools these days encourage children to work on their homework as independently as possible. For instance, Eshan's school has this fabulous thing called academic integrity which teaches the kids to be honest and self-reliant while completing their tasks. The most heartening thing is that the children take it very seriously indeed.

Parents though are a different lot. Let us just admit it. Letting go is not easy and sometimes it is difficult not to sit with our children the entire time that they are doing their assignments and even check every single answer to make sure it is correct. I am no better. Hell, there have been times when I have literally been tempted to snatch the pencil from my son's hand and just scribble the answers myself. The fact that he hates writing and takes an inordinately long time to write five words does not help matters. (Sometimes I think homework is the teacher's way to find out how smart parents are.) Jokes aside, we are not doing our kids any favours by spoon-feeding them. The answer really lies in striking a balance. I try to keep myself updated on the unit of enquiry (the central theme for that particular term) so that I can support whatever is being taught in school with enhancement on the home front. As when they were doing a unit on the universe, we sat down one Sunday afternoon and watched Space Buddies together. Then there was the time they were doing a unit on migratory birds and we arranged a trip to a bird sanctuary with a couple of other kids. There really are such wonderful ways in which we can stay involved with our kids' school lives without intruding into their space or overextending ourselves. All we have to do is focus, prioritise and get the balance right.

And so, the parent–school relationship can be a very, very rewarding one but at the end of the day, every parent would have a different take, a different approach and a different set of circumstances. It also largely depends on what your child wants and how welcoming a particular school is to parent involvement. Speaking for myself, suffice it to say that I love participating wholeheartedly in the annual winter carnival, but would definitely draw the line at volunteering for that monthly Show and Tell.

18

Having Fun with Fitness

How to Get Your Kids to Adapt to Healthy Living

'Adults call it working out. Kids call it playing.'

—Anonymous

Do you know what my first thought is every time my son and I get invited to yet another birthday party? *Another dose of greasy, fat-ridden, unhealthy food for the two of us*! I sometimes cannot help but wonder why almost every birthday party *has* to have such an unhealthy, unwholesome, fat-ridden food menu. Is it like a precondition or something? And let us not even get started about the 2 kg rich chocolate cake with the 3 kg topping of yellow fondant that is bound to get stuck somewhere between your five-year-old's pharynx and oesophagus? Ughhhh!

Do you remember what our grandparents and parents used to say to us when we used to have that rare bowl of instant noodles or a slice of chocolate pastry from the bakery across the road? *Kabhi-kabhi chalta hai*! Well, that is not how it is any more. You see, our lifestyles have changed dramatically over the years and eating out has become the norm rather than the exception. Weekend gala buffets, elaborate birthday parties and other social events have become the order of the day which means that at least once a week (sometimes even more), we and our children have to be subjected to unhealthy food that almost gives me a heart attack just by looking at it. And if I were to be perfectly honest, as far as unhealthy food is concerned, birthday parties really do take the cake! Seriously, sometimes the moment that server arrives with a plateful of fried, cheesy lard and offers it to my child at a birthday party or play date, I feel like just yanking it out of his hands and yelling, 'The country's facing a paediatric obesity epidemic or didn't you notice?'

It is actually strange you know, this complete disregard to health that we witness at children's events. I mean, look at the sheer number of opportunities for all kinds of physical activities that have sprung up practically everywhere. When I was growing up in a busy South Delhi neighbourhood, we were lucky to find a clear space to ride our bicycles in, let alone have access to clubs with pools and tennis courts. These kids are different. They lead pretty golden lives if you consider the kind of activities and opportunities available to them all the time. Tennis, swimming, cycling, soccer, self-defence, basketball, gymnastics and all within easy reach. Then of course, we have tons and tons of information available these days and more and more people getting professionally involved in the health and fitness industry. You would think then, wouldn't you, that with so much more awareness about the importance of good health and fitness out in the open, the situation would have been different and the fried chicken nuggets and butter cookies would have long since been replaced with bell pepper nachos and wholewheat, date and carrot cake? Well, that has not happened and that is why we must accept that this is an issue that needs to be taken gravely and not waved away with a blithe remark such as, 'Young people can eat everything.' In a nutshell, I could not agree more with that age-old adage, 'Healthy habits start early'.

Despite changing circumstances and increasing challenges, we have to keep things interesting and fascinating if we want our kids to stay on track and that goes for fitness as well. And what better example of that is there than the 2020 lockdown? With schools and soccer and swimming (pretty much everything) shut and closed for an indefinite period of time, this mum was positively distraught! I have to tell you about the time when I finally stepped out of my house to go for a simple walk around my complex about fifteen days after the lockdown had been initiated. Even as I tentatively started walking with my mask firmly on, I could not help noticing that almost everyone I saw (albeit from a very, very safe distance) appeared to have gained some weight. This was particularly true of the children and I sighed as I imagined them in front of their computers and tablets, trying to keep themselves occupied within the confines of their homes, poor souls! I realized right then that I would have to think out-of-the-box if I wanted my family not to fall victim to this second (equally worrying) health concern that was also fast threatening to turn into an epidemic.

Now while I have always believed that children's activities should be in the great outdoors as much as possible, we had to make the best of the situation. So even though I would have ideally liked to see my child playing soccer or tennis or going swimming or cycling with his friends, I had to be realistic. But I certainly did not want to leave him to his own devices (pun intended), playing on the laptop all day! Whether that meant downloading a slew of fantastic home workouts (especially curated for kids), or practising yoga every morning with him, or even getting into cooking mode together (we did manage to master some healthy *and* delicious recipes), I knew we had to keep ourselves going. Of course, who had ever expected that the lockdown would go on as indefinitely as it did? But thankfully, between the home workouts, the Physical Education assignments that his school mailed on a regular basis and the cycling around the complex with his dad which was approved by the family doctor as 'relatively safe', we were able to stay on track. The main challenge we faced was how to keep everything consistently innovative since we were dealing with a child. Here are some pointers I have picked up over the years on how, despite all the challenges of modern living, to keep the kids *and* ourselves on track as far as health and fitness are concerned. Read on friends, because, trust me, that triple burger combo with large fries and orange soda that your child gulped down at that amusement park yesterday, is not going to burn itself. So here goes.

Set an example

This is much more effective than I can ever adequately express. Picture this. I am sitting on the couch with a bag of potato wafers, watching a sitcom. My child wanders into the room. 'Eat your carrot sticks and then go do Zumba!' I command. Absurd, isn't it? After all, haven't we heard that famous quote? Practise what you preach. This is even more relevant when we are talking about fitness. We lead by example. If our children see us leading healthy lives and making healthy decisions and choices, they are very likely to do the same. We are the role models for them, so walk the talk. Stop stocking those packets of chips in the house altogether. Accompany your child to the swimming pool and don't forget to take that 'Mama y yo' Zumba class together.

Evenings are for dodgeball, soccer and cycling

I know as children we spent a great deal of our free time playing games like kho-kho or dodgeball in the neighbourhood park with our friends under the twilight sun. Sounds ideal, right? Well, the reality these days is far from it. Things have drastically changed and plenty of kids these days are too hooked on to their tablets and computers to lift their heads and even look out of the windows of their high-rise apartments. Little do they realize that other than serious neck, shoulder and eyesight problems, they are also in grave danger of another very serious side effect—a huge backside! Prising them away from technology may not always be easy but we have to try. Set limits on time they can spend on the computer. Get them interested in cycling and swimming and other outdoor physical activities. Participate in your local marathon and take your child along. Enrol them in their school's after-hours sports club. It is amazing how many parents I have met who grumble about their children's academic performance sliding because of too many co-curricular activities and then turn a blind eye when their wards waste away entire weekends, tapping away mindlessly on some electronic device or the other.

Eat something before you go for those ghastly birthday parties

Okay, I know that this is a very, very specific tip but sometimes that is exactly what you need. Suffice it to say that the chocolate fountain and crazy candy corner at your child's best friend's party may have looked pretty swanky, but their effects on your child's body is going to be pretty costly too. So the thing is, if we don't want our children to be feasting on that kind of stuff, we are going to have to make a plan. Mine usually involves a giant banana or a pile of wholewheat, home-made pancakes just before we leave for the party. I make sure that both of us dig (well and truly) into this healthy, wholesome snack before we go, and voila! You can place the craziest candy corner in front of us and we will still smile beatifically and politely shake our heads. Okay, I am exaggerating, just a little bit. However, this does ensure that we don't gorge ourselves on every lard-ridden, fat-infused fiend that is plonked down on our unsuspecting plates. Translation? Eat that humble banana before you get out. It works.

Check out the urban akhada in your neighbourhood

It is amazing how simple creativity and thought can transform the concept of a family outing into something enjoyable and wholesome. Now that does not mean that I am against visiting a video game or go-carting arcade or even the super pizza joint that recently opened its doors and offers a 25 per cent discount for children's birthday parties. It is just that those do not have to be the undisputed venue choices every single time. There are plenty of new concepts springing up everywhere these days, concepts which explore the possibility of children having hearty, healthy, wholesome fun in the great outdoors (or even indoors). Whether that is a farm full of animals where the kids can feed the chickens, ride on the horses and play with the dogs followed by a lunch prepared fresh on the farm, or an urban *akhada* kind of place where they can chase each other, climb ropes and jump over tires thereby expending every single ounce of spare physical energy they have got, or even the spanking new studio which organizes the most amazing dance parties for kids, the bottom line is to start having fun with fitness and get the children moving.

19

Time to Upgrade

How to Bring up Tech-savvy Kids

> 'It takes them half an hour to tie their shoelaces and only 12 seconds to troubleshoot the iPad.'
>
> —Anonymous

I think my child's first brush with technology happened when he was two years old. There was this app called Talking Tom which was quite a cool thing actually and very, very effective at keeping children calm and happy. It was a cat with a funny little voice and it imitated anything you said. Eshan was crazy about it, and I used it to calm and distract him in many a difficult situation. And I am certainly not alone. Haven't we all seen that toddler on a flight or in a restaurant being tossed a smartphone just to keep him quiet so that the mum or dad can sit back and breathe for a few seconds? Now I do agree that it might have been more responsible parenting to at least *try* to calm a screaming child with some soothing music or a story instead, but somehow the smartphone just seemed to be the most effective option. Come on, you agree, don't you? Admit it!

Let me mention right at the outset that I was never the kind of mum who was averse to technology. I mean, even schools have information and computer technology (ICT) classes and regularly use smartboards and iPads for young children these days. However, I was not the completely cool kind either. I guess I was somewhere in between. You know, the kind who would allow the use of a laptop or smartphone for a limited amount of time as long as I could effectively monitor what Eshan was doing with it, and prioritise things like outdoor activities, music and reading time.

Now while technology has been an integral part of our lives for many years, there is no disputing the fact that it did get elevated to a whole new status during the Covid pandemic. It would not be an exaggeration to say that our sanity, even our survival, depended on technology back then. Think about it! All those Zoom meetings and webinars and videoconferences. How could we have managed without them? Not to mention those online classes for the children. In fact, if anyone managed to seamlessly, painlessly, acclimatize to technology during the pandemic, it was our children. Even as I think about it now, one particular instance immediately comes to mind.

The lockdown was on and my nine-year-old son was in an online class. Suddenly, he came running up to me and said urgently, 'My audio got glitched!'

'How do you even know that word?' I muttered as I ran to help him.

Frankly, I am not very hands-on with computer apps or anything to do with tech really. While I have been using laptops and smartphones for years, before I became a mother my rule as far as technology goes was to know things strictly on a 'need-to-know' basis. So much so that I think the six-month National Institute of Information Technology (NIIT) course I signed up for in college was completely wasted on me. Anyway, as far as the audio was concerned, eventually Eshan figured it out on his own. I have to admit I was mighty impressed when I saw his small fingers fly across the keyboard. He pressed something, then something else and voila! He had managed to fix the problem. Then there was the time when he even managed to help me fix something. I was working on an office presentation and was trying to save a Word file on the desktop. Pretty basic, right? The computer though did not think so and it kept displaying an error message. That is when Eshan walked in and nonchalantly said, 'You've opened too many apps, Mum. Close them and then try and save it.'

I looked at him in amazement, then tried what he had suggested, and lo and behold! It worked! That was the day I fully realized just how tech-savvy this generation really is.

These children have been using laptops and iPads long before they even learnt to read. They are matter of fact, blasé and relaxed around technology. Of course, now with so much focus on online learning and digital classrooms and everything, plus a lot of our own work revolving around technology and many of us working from home, we parents don't really have a choice but to embrace this double-edged sword. Truth be told, I have to admit that I was infinitely thankful to technology during the Covid-19 lockdown. Puneet and I were able to work effectively and my child was constructively engaged for five hours every day in online classes. Even his tae kwon do and abacus classes were happening digitally. Undoubtedly, it was what helped me keep my sanity and it was with a feeling of deep gratitude that I sat down to grasp the technicalities of platforms like MS Teams and Zoom.

Admittedly, when Eshan worked out that technical glitch for my presentation, the thought did cross my mind that when it comes to technology, my child might be the one helping me, not the other way round. And I am certainly not alone. A recent survey found out that a significant percentage of parents actually learn the use of several electronic devices and apps from their children. The survey further revealed that in more ways than we can even hope to count, our children are far ahead of us in all matters related to technology. The point is, are we okay with that? Do we want to be the people who turn a blind eye to what our kids are doing on those laptops simply because we can't figure it out?

We all know that technology is a double-edged sword. I have a friend whose husband owns a web-designing company. It did seem a little strange to me when she told me that her son is allowed the least amount of screen time among his peer group. 'His father is very firm about it,' she remarked. Later when I thought about it, it made sense to me. He was in the business; who would know the dangers and menaces of this world better than him? Even though as parents of younger children, things like social media and digital porn are not things we are currently dealing with, it is never too early to acquaint ourselves with the challenges of bringing children up in the digital age.

Speaking from my own experience, I have to confess that Puneet and I seriously considered getting a camera installed in Eshan's room after he got his first laptop. It was soon after a frenzy over an extremely dangerous online game happened, and we were very, very concerned. Later we googled the game and was it scary or what? Within a matter of seconds, the computer screen was swarmed with countless articles and websites with warnings on the dangers of online gaming and how young children were falling prey to it. The title of a particularly frightening article on a popular parenting website was '7 Dangerous Games Parents Must Know About'.

When we were growing up, our parents warned us about the dangers of things like drugs and alcohol but certainly not 'games'. When we were children, 'games' meant kho-kho, hopscotch and freeze tag. Not to say that we did not play video games, of course we did. I distinctly remember one that I was quite addicted to. It was called Islander, I think. Nice and friendly it was, and certainly nothing like some of the stuff the kids play these days. But things were different back then. Addiction, sleep disorders, eye strain, neck and back problems, reduced attention span, behavioural issues—these were not things our parents had to really worry about. Then there are the more dangerous evils stalking the internet like cyberbullying, privacy problems, online predators, malware—the list is quite long.

I am sure there are many of us out there who are very tech-savvy and can easily be that mum or dad who can remotely turn off the child's computer. Some of you, particularly able ones, might even be able to fix your child's phone or set up a Tumblr for them to upload those stop-motion videos. But there are also some like me. Parents who may not be complete geeks but need to know enough to be able to speak our kids' language to some extent, and monitor and supervise them to ensure that they stay safe in that big, bad world out there. Did you know that there are quite a number of parent tech workshops which can prove to be a blessing for parents like us? Designed to help parents understand the role of social media in a youngster's life, how to respond to cyberbullying and digital porn, and set healthy limits on video games, etc., these workshops are just what the doctor ordered and will help you become exactly what you need to be to keep up with your children. A tech-savvy parent! In a nutshell, a parent who understands (or at least can effectively *pretend* to understand) exactly what their child is doing on that fiendish little tablet or laptop. A parent who stays updated on what is going on but does not allow technology to completely govern the way we live our lives.

Here are some of the things that a tech-savvy parent does to monitor, supervise and help the child adopt a balanced approach to everything that whizzes.

Set an example

Like everything else, leading by example is the best strategy here too. Whether we like to admit it or not, parents are just as bad about excessive screen time as the kids. We see them all the time, you know, parents who are strict as ever about how much time their children can spend on a video game or show on an OTT platform, while they themselves sit up until the wee hours of the morning, binge watching that new series on their iPads! '*I'm* your mother, you're not my mother!' Now we may get away with that kind of thing for a while but sooner or later, our children are bound to question the discrimination. And why should they not? Our children look for role models they can follow, role models that lead by example. Show your child that there is more to life than non-stop online chatting, social media updates and emails. Show them that you can successfully put away that mobile phone into the darkest corner of the drawer without succumbing to temptation. Set an example that they can proudly follow.

Stay updated on technology being used in school

Schools are becoming increasingly tech-savvy, preparing kids for the fast-paced, technology-based world out there. We need to stay abreast with technology that is being used at school because it will bring us up to speed with what our kids are doing. And frankly, if the school is using a particular app or programme, it has obviously been well and truly substantiated and is probably safe. A great example of this would be the online classes that happened during the lockdown. Eshan's school was using MS Teams (a safe and secure platform) to conduct classes and since all classwork and homework were being uploaded there, I had to acquaint myself with every feature that the platform had to offer. Not only did this help me stay in touch with his schoolwork, I became so adept at using MS Teams that I was comfortably able to use it for my own work meetings as well. And yes, being familiar with the platform ensured that Eshan knew that I was aware of what was going on. Other than a couple of stray incidents, he basically toed the line.

Set screen time limits and don't forget to converse with your children

'Mum, five minutes more.'

'I said no!'

'Okay then, how about two minutes more?'

Sounds familiar? Hard as it is, don't relent. Staying firm is the answer to this all-too-common situation. Stick to the daily pre-determined limit. One thing I am also very particular about is not using screen time to reward or discipline. Naturally though, staying firm does not mean that we close all channels of communication. Our kids are smarter and wiser than we give them credit for. Talk to them about the advantages and disadvantages of being online. Tell them about the dangers of online predators and how violent TV shows, movies and video games can affect their minds. Give them practical reasons and examples that they will relate to. That is the only way they will be able to understand the reasons behind the rules and restrictions. Listen to their opinions as well. There is a lot of pressure out there to 'be with it' and the world is getting increasingly relentless as we speak. Mutual understanding and open communication can really go a long way in building trust which is a prerequisite as far as safe use of technology is concerned.

Encourage technology for educational purposes

Most kids will want to have some screen time. Why not use it to your advantage by focusing on some of the more constructive apps and programs? There are so many of those out there that we are literally spoilt for choice: Reading apps with extensive e-book libraries, apps with maths games featuring fundamental skills and concepts, language learning, geography, coding and programming, logic puzzles to enhance problem-solving skills—and it can go on and on and on. Even time reserved for television can be steered towards educational programmes which can prove to be a treasure trove of information and knowledge. So, make the best of the situation.

Having said that, setting aside some time for device-free activities is very important as well. Whether it is activities like sports or music or reading, or even family time in the evening when everyone sits together and tells each other about the happenings of the day, some device-free time (and this goes for *your* mobile phones too) should be a part of your children's daily schedule. I have a colleague who never allows devices to accompany any meal in her house; mealtime in her house is strictly device-free time. Although her kids and even her husband protested for a while, eventually they got used to it and started enjoying the lively conversations that gradually became a tradition in their house.

Track, blog and stay informed

There are some very useful tools out there to help parents monitor tech devices and set time and content restrictions. Most routers, web browsers and TVs have effective parental controls which can give some much–needed security and peace of mind to parents. If the children are using smartphones, there are settings and apps that will help you create filters. Joining and following parenting blogs and groups are a great way to share information and get advice from other parents who also face the all-pervasive problem of bringing up children in a tech-crazy world. And don't let the guard down. Speaking for myself, I like to stay informed and on top of what my son is doing with technology, from the shows he watches, to the games he plays, to the people he interacts with.

Finally, don't over-restrict

I have always believed that trust is at the core of a healthy parent–child relationship or for that matter any relationship. That relates to their friends, to their studies and even to technology. Sometimes over-restricting or over-controlling can do more harm than good. It is like the forbidden fruit logic. You naturally hanker after what you cannot get. Very often children of those parents who over-restrict the tech part tend to be more curious about it and may conceal what they are doing from their parents. Isn't it better to have a transparent relationship and be aware of what is going on? And honestly, we do tend to over-think the tech part, don't we? Let us aim for balance. After all, do we want our children to lag behind while other children are designing their own websites and participating in coding competitions and what not? Despite all its issues, technology has become an intrinsic part of our lives now and will continue to be, so why not learn to live graciously with it? Here is what we need to understand—not all tech is bad and not everyone is out to get our kids and us. If we stop inappropriate content, stay in touch and talk to our children, we will do just fine.

In Conclusion

> 'The days are long. But the years are short.'
>
> —Gretchen Rubin

When I started writing this book, I took myself back to the beginning, to the day my son was born. Reliving the past through the chapters has been a truly wonderful and enriching experience for me. Every stage of motherhood has been fantastic in its own special way. Now I am the mother of a twelve-year-old boy in whom I can already see glimpses of a fine, young man in the making. This child of mine might still be the boy who comes running up to me, expecting me to kiss his knee when he hurts it while cycling down in the park, but he is also the first one at the dining table to offer me a glass of water when I have a choking fit and the first one to put his arms around me and comfort me when I am upset. It is at moments like these that I truly realize how much has changed since the first time I held him in my arms. The one who has not changed as much as she should have is me. I used to peep into his room and check on him six times a night and I still do it. Well, maybe not as much. I am down to three times on a good night these days.

Now even though we might want things to stay as wonderfully dreamy as before, the reality is (and this may sound terribly cliched) that children grow up much faster than their parents would ideally like them to. From tiny, kicking, bawling beings, they shoot up into independent, capable young adults, eager to make their places in the world. The people who stay constant throughout this evolution are the parents. We thought we knew best, we still do. We worried constantly, we still do. We stayed up at night, we still do. I am no exception, but I cannot help thinking that perhaps it really might be time for me to get a little perspective and give that child of mine some credit. A child still, yes, and perhaps always, at least for me, but with a strong, capable mind of his own. After all, he did manage to give me a wonderfully insightful viewpoint on global warming and climate change, didn't he? Maybe he really is smarter and more capable than I realized.

Bitter-sweet. A word that just did not figure in my dictionary until I became a mother. Let me explain. The first couple of years were busy yet peacefully uneventful, and I thank God for that. However, my first proper brush with the word *bitter-sweet* happened the day Eshan started preschool and I watched him being led away by a relative stranger. The proud feeling of allowing him to make his first tiny steps into the world coupled with the heartbreaking realization of being away from him, of not being able to see him or touch him for four long hours. Bitter-sweet indeed. And that was just the beginning. Now the past twelve years seem to have gone by far too quickly.

I remember a friend who happily gave up a glittering career as a partner in a law firm to bring up her two children. Once she wholeheartedly threw herself into the role of mother-of-two, she never looked back. The years rushed past much too quickly and suddenly she was packing a bag for her younger daughter, getting ready to send her off to college to the other end of the world.

'That's when it hit me,' she confessed to me one day. 'They'd both grown up, I had not. I'd never completely understood the meaning of the term "empty nest syndrome" until that day. That's when I fully realized the enormity of the situation. That's when I realized that I needed to grow up too.'

I had a similar experience recently too, though my child is still young, thank goodness. So even though there is still plenty of time to even think about packing his bags for college, there has been some tentative talk in our house recently about the possibility of Eshan going on a school camp. Now this may not seem like such a big deal to any random person who hears about it, but ask a mother. To her, it is not just a school camp, to her it means being deprived of the opportunity to kiss her child goodnight; to her it is about constantly, continuously, incessantly worrying through those two sleepless nights, imagining and dreading things that can only come to a mother's mind. And more than anything, to her it is a confirmation of her worst fears.

That her child really is growing up at an alarmingly fast pace, a pace that she simply cannot keep up with.

'Let them grow up. Equip them, prepare them to face the world on their own.'

'Let them face small disappointments. Be there but don't mollycoddle all the time.'

'Be a parent but be a friend as well. A friend who truly understands.'

Pearls of wisdom, all of them. Yet, difficult to implement. So difficult. Imagine that fight in the playground. That misunderstanding in school. That maths quiz where someone else was chosen instead of him. It can take all your self-control not to intervene, to allow your child to resolve it himself, to fight his own battles. It can be difficult, if not impossible, not to allow emotions to get in the way, not to shield, protect and shelter your precious one from every hardship that comes along. That is what we have been doing until now and it is hard to change that. Hard to accept that the little girl with pigtails who held your hand and walked to school every single morning for the past ten years, really is old enough to board the school bus on her own now. Or that the little boy who needed you to accompany him to every single birthday party is now capable enough to be dropped off for a movie with his friends. Needless to say that he can also choose his own clothes, make his bed, decide whether he wants to play soccer or tennis, and handle his own relationships. Can he also decide whether he wants broccoli or a candy bar for his evening snack? Or whether he can have an extra hour of screen time on Sundays? Okay, admittedly I will be drawing the line there. Still plenty of time for that. Let us not push it too far, eh?

This section has no elegant coffee silhouettes. It has no tips, no easy pointers, no general advice, no suggestions on how best to deal with a situation that each of us has to face at some point. Letting go. Allowing our children to grow up. Accepting. Because unlike everything else, there really is no easy way to do that. You see, we play this role to the best of our abilities far too long to suddenly be able to stop. So much so that it almost becomes second nature to us to worry, over-think, over-analyse and solve pretty much everything, all the time. I am sure you must have heard the famous quote: *God made mothers because He couldn't be everywhere himself.*

It should come as no surprise then that we get used to putting our children first, prioritising them over everything else. It is no wonder that suddenly reclaiming our lives back as they used to be, and allowing our kids to discover theirs, well, it certainly is not easy or simple. How can it be? How can I get used to the fact that the child who would call me thirty times in the middle of an important workday, really does not need me for every single thing any more? How can I come to terms with the fact that I can now book an overnight work trip and go back to making my own plans for the weekend, when what I really want to do is to take the evening flight back so that I can attend another crazy superhero-themed birthday party with Eshan?

Okay, that one is actually unbelievable, even to my own ears. The thing is, this is not about the friends we are no longer in touch with because we wanted to spend the evenings at home reading Brer Rabbit instead, or the careers we did not prioritise because we wanted to be around to kiss that bruised knee or attend that open house at school. It is not about the parties we missed because we wanted to do something as minor as fix that cup of bedtime hot chocolate, or those anniversaries that we preferred to spend at that family restaurant with the candy corner instead of at a fancy candlelit dinner. Basically, it is not about a feeling of having sacrificed or given up, because that is not what true love is about. It has more to do with looking back at that beautiful time with pride and love and then figuring out how to re-connect with ourselves, now that we are no longer on call 24/7.

Not to say that our children do not need us any more, of course they do. It is just that the needs are now different as is the role we play in their lives, as they get ready to spread their wings and learn to fly. And yes, it is about flying ourselves once again too. Sometimes we fly together, sometimes we go our different ways. Sometimes we return to the same nests, sometimes they make new ones. But the love stays. The love always stays, the bond getting stronger and stronger as the years go by. This unique bond that is like no other. This blessed bond that has been bestowed on us like a precious gift that we will treasure and cherish forever. This beautiful bond between mother and child.

Acknowledgements

'Sometimes the strength of motherhood is greater than natural laws.'

This quote by Barbara Kingsolver struck a chord with me the first time I read it. I think it summarizes everything that I know about motherhood and each one of its amazing, magical hues.

When I started writing this book, I knew that it was going to be an extremely emotional and enriching experience for me. After all, I was chronicling a very special, very precious journey. A mother's journey. All the joy, all the love, all the beautiful irrationality, all the fears, all the sleepless nights. Straight from one mum to another mum. A journey that will bring a smile to every mother's face.

First and foremost, I want to express my deepest gratitude to my brilliant literary agent, mentor and friend, Suhail Mathur of The Book Bakers. Suhail is truly agent extraordinaire. His support, guidance, faith and confidence have played a tremendous role in the journey of this book. Thank you, Suhail, for everything that you do.

My sincere gratitude to my dynamic publisher, Ajay Mago of Om Books International for welcoming me into the Om Books family with so much warmth. It is truly a pleasure and a privilege to work with you. Thank you for giving me an opportunity to share this fascinating journey with the world.

My heartfelt thanks to Editor-in-Chief Shantanu Ray Chaudhuri for providing an extremely enriching learning experience. I am truly grateful for your encouragement as well as your invaluable insights. Thank you for being such a fabulous inspiration.

A huge thank you to my editor, Jyotsna Mehta, for her superb inputs and diligent attention to every detail. Working with a committed and talented editor like you has been a pleasure all the way!

It takes a village to bring a child up. I could not agree more. There are so many people who have supported me, stood by me and held me up during this phenomenal journey of motherhood.

My husband Puneet who has been a true partner in every sense of the word. Suffice it to say that watching him levelling up so seamlessly and beautifully from husband to father has touched my heart more than I can ever express.

And of course my son, Eshan, I love you.

My father Swapn for not only being the greatest dad in the world, but also being the most awesome grandfather I know. He has been a marvellous best friend and a tremendous inspiration to my son over the years.

My mum Shirley who undertook the brand new role of a grandmother quite effortlessly! To see her grow to love someone as much as she has always loved me has been an experience like no other.

My grandmother Deepa. Though she is no more, she lives on in the amazing memories we created together over the years. She showered Eshan with more love than I could have ever imagined. One day I will tell him how lucky he was to have known her.

My maternal aunt Punam. Thank you for everything you have done to make the days (and the nights!) easier for Eshan and me. Your love and support are precious.

To my family and all my lovely friends. It has been absolutely wonderful to share these treasured years with you.

And finally, an enormous thank you to you, my incredible readers. Your love and faith mean the world to me. After all, I write because you read.